Finding Words for Worship

Finding Words for Worship

A Guide for Leaders

RUTH C. DUCK

Westminster John Knox Press
Louisville, Kentucky

Scripture quotations from the New Revised Standard Version of the Bible are copyright © 1989 by the Division of Christian Education of the National Council of the Churches of Christ in the U.S.A. and are used by permission.

Book design by Publishers' WorkGroup
Cover design by Kim Wohlenhaus

First edition

Published by Westminster John Knox Press
Louisville, Kentucky

This book is printed on acid-free paper that meets the American National Standards Institute Z39.48 standard. ∞

PRINTED IN THE UNITED STATES OF AMERICA

95 96 97 98 99 00 01 02 03 04 — 10 9 8 7 6 5 4 3 2 1

Library of Congress Cataloging-in-Publication Data

Duck, Ruth C., 1947–
    Finding words for worship : a guide for leaders / Ruth C. Duck.
        p.   cm.
    Includes bibliographical references.
    ISBN 0-664-25573-6 (alk. paper)
    1. Public worship. 2. Liturgies. 3. Worship programs.
BV10.2.D83 1995
264'.0014—dc20   95-19389

Contents

Preface   vii

1. Finding Words for Worship   1

2. The Creative Process   10

3. Disciplines of Writing for Worship   20

4. Finding Images for Worship   33

5. Finding Words to Preach   45

6. Forms of Prayer and Worship   62

7. Thanksgiving at Table:
Prayers for Holy Communion   88

8. Finding Words to Sing   102

9. Bringing It All Together   119

Notes   133

Preface

In my beginning worship classes, I ask students to prepare written prayers. I respond to the prayers with written feedback. Then they have the opportunity to rewrite them. A few days ago a student told me, "I'm anxious about this assignment. It's hard for me to find the words to express what I want to say in a prayer." The path toward developing a relationship with God or helping congregations express their worship is a meandering country road, not a shortcut or a superhighway. Yet the church is not without maps, compasses, or guides in the journey toward renewing corporate prayer. In this book, I seek to present methods, disciplines, and models that can help congregations find words for worship—words that come out of the creativity and contemporary life of Christians.

This book is meant primarily as a resource for persons who design services and who write their own prayers, hymns, or sermons. It also may serve those who seek a deeper understanding of the parts of worship involving words. Understanding the creative disciplines that are needed to prepare prayers, hymns, and sermons may also provide help in evaluating resources already available. It may also be useful as a survey and theological interpretation of the spoken parts of worship.

This book is for laity, clergy, and seminarians. It is for artisans of the word and for persons who evaluate, adapt, or assemble words already available for worship. It is for persons of varied Christian denominations, in areas where they have local freedom and responsibility for developing words of worship. For example, Roman Catholics are certain and United Methodists are likely to use approved texts for Holy Communion, whereas United Church of Christ pastors seldom use such texts in their entirety, and Disciples of Christ elders often pray extemporaneously. Within one denomination, one church may follow denominational worship books; another may write prayers locally; and still another will pray extemporaneously. Further, occasions outside regular Sunday worship often call for local worship design, no matter what the denomination. Thus different chapters will serve leaders of different churches in various ways.

Admittedly, freshly created words are only one aspect of worship. The shape of the room in which worship happens and the use of color, form, and symbolism within it powerfully influence the experience of worship. The taste and texture of communion bread, movement and stillness in the room, the smell of candles or evergreen branches, and the touch of hands extended in welcome all shape Christian worship. Silence, too, can be a vivid dimension of worship. Clearly, worship involves more than words.

This book, then, addresses only one aspect of worship: words spoken or sung. It seems that the Spirit has given me a gift for finding words for worship, expressed through writing worship resources and hymns. In recent years, I have become interested in helping others develop their creative gifts in writing for worship. Groups have asked me to lead workshops on "creative worship." The title irritated me; I imagined they wanted to hear about innovations or gimmicks that make worship appear contemporary but that may not deepen corporate prayer. Then I realized that the title "creative worship" reflected a desire to discover creative gifts in writing for worship, and I began to design workshops to serve that purpose. This book grows out of many such workshops, seminars, and classes.

It would be impossible to name all the people whose support, ideas, and suggestions have contributed to this book. A few warrant special mention. Horace Allen, my adviser in the field of worship in the doctor of theology program at Boston University School of Theology, is a source of valuable information but, even more, a mentor in developing my historical, theological, and pastoral analysis of worship. My good friend Rebecca Ferguson, who by the time this book is published will have completed her Ph.D. in English from

Marquette University, has provided me with many ideas and resources about writing over the years. Neal Fisher, the president of Garrett-Evangelical Theological Seminary, supported the work by approving a sabbatical, as well as funding editorial assistance, ably provided by Ph.D. student Dori Baker. Linda Koops, administrative secretary to the faculty, has provided valuable assistance of various kinds, including training in various word processing and computer skills.

Several people helped by giving me feedback on drafts of the manuscript. Hoyt Hickman, who for many years has provided leadership in the field of worship for the United Methodist Church's Board of Discipleship, read the entire manuscript and provided invaluable suggestions, as did Dori Baker. I sought the help of two groups in working on parts of chapter 6 (the act of confession, the prayers of the people, and the pastoral prayer): The Garrett-Evangelical Theological Seminary faculty, who attended my sabbatical report in October 1994, and a group of church leaders from the North Indiana Conference, United Methodist Church, who participated in a seminar I led in November 1994. Their ideas contributed richly to that chapter. Donald F. Chatfield, professor of preaching at Garrett-ETS, provided bibliographical resources for chapter 6 and helpful commentary on chapter 5.

I appreciate the wise counsel of Cynthia Thompson, who was my editor at Westminster John Knox Press as the book was being developed. I am also pleased that Stephanie Egnotovich, who once before at another press helped me finish a book I had started with another editor, was able to help me complete this project.

The Holy Spirit is the prime teacher in the school of prayer (Rom. 8:26). This book will have succeeded if, beyond all the theoretical and practical advice it contains, it points readers toward the holy source of all true worship and all true creativity. To God be glory now and always!

1

Finding Words
for Worship

Words are an important part of worship, as a complement to dimensions of worship involving movement, the visual, music without words, and silence. Finding words to express praise, prayer, and proclamation is worthy of loving and reverent care. Some words may come from liturgies of the past or from denominational worship books; others may overflow spontaneously out of present life. Still others may be prepared and written out in advance and printed in a worship program as a guide for a congregation's participation. Words for worship that are prepared locally are the focus of this book; I begin by exploring the role of such words in relation to other dimensions of worship.

Forms of Participation
in Worship

Words for worship that are prepared locally build on the language, rhythms, and concerns of traditional and denominational liturgies. When I was a beginning pastor learning how to lead congregations in prayer, the psalms (those ancient liturgies) and *The Book of Common Prayer* were my teachers. My study of liturgical history has suggested rich possibilities for worship today—from celebrating the ancient Easter vigil to beginning a communion hymn with an image from the Didache, a Christian document from first or second century Syria. Yet emerging theological insights and human concerns often call for revision of past liturgies or creation of new ones.

In recent years, denominational liturgies have undergone significant reform, making them more appropriate for local church worship. In 1974 when I first became a pastor in the United Church of Christ, I had great difficulty using the baptism service in the hymnal.[1] Its main scripture reference was to Jesus' welcome of the children—not, in my opinion, a baptismal text. The 1986 United Church of Christ *Book of Worship* provides baptismal texts that are far more theologically sound, drawing on richly diverse New Testament baptismal texts.[2] Many denominations have made similar reforms in services for baptism and Holy Communion. Newer denominational liturgies attend more to vivid symbolism, inclusive language, and varied liturgical needs. Denominational hymnals, worship books, and supplements can be excellent resources for worship in the local church.

Since denominational liturgies are developed after much study and debate and then carefully edited and tested, they may surpass the work of individual persons. Used over years, they enrich a congregation's memory and nourish their spirituality. I used the following prayer in graveside services for fifteen years:

> O Lord, support us all the day long of this troublous life, until the shadows lengthen and the evening comes, and the busy world is hushed, and the fever of life is over, and our work is done. Then of thy tender mercy grant us a safe lodging, and a holy rest, and peace at the last; through Jesus Christ our Lord. Amen.[3]

How moving it was to mouth these words by heart along with my mother's pastor when he repeated them beside her grave.

Liturgies that live over time nurture Christian memories; and liturgies that are the same throughout a denomination help people feel at home wherever they are—in a new home or on vacation. And, since denominations have learned from one another in designing orders for Holy Communion, baptism, marriage, and other services, Christians often recognize common structures and texts when visiting a church of another denomination. Denominational liturgies have many advantages; locally written resources for worship should ordinarily complement rather than replace them.

Spontaneity also supports vital and engaging worship. Our most memorable worship experiences may be the most spontaneous. Some years ago, two of us were sprinkling water on a large congregation during a baptismal renewal service, while the organist played an exquisite rendering of an Easter hymn, "Now the green blade rises." I was concentrating on sprinkling water on everyone in my rows, and I did not notice that my partner was lagging behind. In frustration, he tried to cover territory more quickly by propelling larger amounts of water over a greater distance. His generous gesture sent ripples of laughter through the congregation. This spontaneous moment stands out to me as a revelation of Easter joy in worship. Most people who participate regularly in Christian worship treasure memories of such spontaneous moments.

Spontaneity is central in some worshiping traditions, for example, in many African American congregations. In such worshiping contexts, both pastors and laity learn how to pray extemporaneously. Freedom from the scripted word brings immediacy to preaching; and the ability to break into song in joyful response to God releases wellsprings of praise. Such congregations expect the Spirit to inspire heartfelt worship. Such services involve preparation—preparation of persons more than words. A daily life of prayer and commitment is the best preparation for spontaneous participation in Christian corporate worship.

Every worship service should leave room for unprogrammed expressions of heartfelt praise and human concern. Traditions that do not highly value spontaneity can learn from those that do. A colleague of mine was guest preacher and worship leader in a church that closely followed a denominational liturgy. The pattern was so rigid that church leaders did not inform their guest leader when someone had a heart attack during the service. How much better it would have been to stop and pray for the sick member. Sometimes our eyes are so glued to our bulletins and hymnals that no one would notice a visitation of angels!

Craig Douglas Erickson, Presbyterian liturgical scholar and author of *Participating in Worship,* has argued that truly participatory worship involves six key elements: (1) silence; (2) involvement through the senses; (3) lay leadership; (4) "interiorized verbal participation" (parts committed to memory, like the prayer at my mother's graveside); (5) "prophetic verbal participation"; and (6) spontaneous participation. This book relates especially to Erickson's category of "prophetic verbal participation," those elements of worship selected or composed through the creativity of individuals entrusted with naming a congregation's daily concerns before God and interpreting God's word to the congregation.[4]

Erickson believes that the prophetic voice should speak primarily through sermons; he fears that locally created prayers may overemphasize the voice of one person, the pastor.[5] To some extent I agree. Locally designed and printed resources should normally be a small part of any given service. Still, the creative, contemporary, contextualized voice contributes vitally to worship. Erickson acknowledges that "the call of the community to prophetic ministry through liturgical leadership is a tremendous gift of freedom in the Spirit," an important gift when used responsibly "with energy, imagination, intelligence, and, above all else, love."[6] When balanced appropriately with other dimensions of worship, written prayers that are created locally can enrich Christian worship. This book is intended to support informed and creative lay and clergy leadership to develop and refine what Erickson calls "prophetic verbal participation." While creating words for worship locally is not without pitfalls, it is an essential part of worship, when responsibly done.

The Creative Contemporary
Voice in Worship

Through the creative voice, worship can address the contexts of life and ministry that face a particular congregation at a particular time. Worship that is contextualized through the creative voice supports a congregation's daily lives and ministries of justice, peace, and witness in the world. This happens when the diversity of local voices sounds— when both laity and clergy speak, and when clergy listen intently to what people are saying about their lives and how they are saying it.

Voices the church has silenced in the past have now begun to speak. Women and laity are finding a voice; some churches now call forth the voices of children. Churches in diverse cultures around the world are seeking ways to incarnate the Christian faith in worship through expressions integral to culture. Such voices are seldom heard in traditional and denominational liturgies. Nurturing the creative voice of the broad spectrum of Christians is an urgent task—both to do simple justice and to express the fullness of Christian praise and prayer.

Particular occasions may call for new words for worship. Over the years, congregations have asked me to write orders to install officers, to commission people involved in Central America solidarity work, and to recognize a scouting program. I could not find printed resources for any of these occasions and had to develop my own. Local church leaders must often develop resources for such occasions. Through the creative voice these occasions can become times of praise and renewed commitment, done with integrity, and not just perfunctory exercises.

It is difficult to trust one's own creativity, to remain open to images and symbols emerging out of one's journey with the Spirit. Many of us have learned to discount our own perceptions, our own truths, especially if we have grown up in families where we were abused and silenced or in schools where every peg was supposed to fit in the same sized hole. We may have internalized social values that deny women's right to shape the language of prayer; or, we may have believed the myth that real men don't develop their creativity. Perhaps, too, we have accepted values that keep us too busy to cultivate a relationship with God or to listen to truths emerging within us. Finding our own creative voice, surfacing our own images, experiences, and perceptions, can be difficult, yet rewarding.

Each person is creative in different ways, but everyone can be creative in some way; the gifts of the Spirit are for all Christians. Elizabeth O'Connor writes: "Our obedience and surrender to God are in large part our obedience and surrender to our gifts. This is the message . . . of the parable of the talents. Our gifts are on loan. We are responsible for spending them in the world."[7] Developing a gift for words, whether as central to one's creativity or as a less central but necessary part of ministry, supports worship with integrity and interest.

Scripture and the Creative Voice

The creative voice in Christian worship expresses contemporary concerns; yet it also draws on the words of scripture. Scripture is central to Christian worship. The words of scripture echo through opening words of praise, hymns, and prayers, as well as through sermons. Official denominational books of worship weave scriptural images and phrases into prayers that echo through decades or centuries. Phyllis Bird, in her book *The Bible as the Church's Book,* notes that the General Prayer of Confession found in *The Book of Common Prayer* and in United Methodist orders of worship alludes to no less than twelve books of the Bible.[8] Erik Routley discovered references to passages from twelve books of the Bible in Charles Wesley's hymn, "Hark! The Herald Angels Sing."[9] Most Protestant churches echo the words, images, and narratives of scripture in extemporaneous and locally created prayer. Worship is the primary context in which the church enters into dialogue with scripture; and scripture is a resource shared across the denominations of Christianity.

Through the creative voice, the concerns, narratives, and images of scripture dialogue with contemporary experience. This is a partial answer to feminists who find the Bible to be a thoroughly patriarchal document that reflects the values of cultures in which men have power over women and women are devalued. Their critique is justified: Men wrote most of scripture; men selected the canon; men have devised lectionaries for scripture reading in worship. The committee that revised the Common Lectionary in 1992, included only one woman as a full member, though consulting with several women.[10]

Scriptures were written in the context of patriarchal society. Patriarchal attitudes are intertwined at the roots with witness to the grace and justice of God—as impossible to separate as the wheat and tares of parable. I do not wish to apologize for scripture, to gloss over its frequently negative attitudes toward women, or to suggest that any particular scripture passage must be accepted as authoritative truth beyond human questioning. Yet women must take part in interpreting scripture, not only as biblical scholars but as worship leaders who bring scripture into dialogue with human experience.

The metaphor of dialogue—involving both active listening and honest expression of our own experience—points toward my understanding of scripture.[11] As the primary written source for the witness to God's presence among humans, especially in Jesus Christ, scripture has a word to speak to Christians. Active listening means attending carefully to what is said, asking questions to deepen our understanding of the world of meaning behind the words. Commentaries can clarify what questions the text was addressing, the audience to which it was speaking, and the nuances of the words the author chose. Simply reading a passage aloud can help us listen more attentively.

But dialogue is more than listening. Only by voicing our honest thoughts and feelings can dialogue go forward. Silencing ourselves or others in pretended agreement is no shortcut to a common mind, as persons engaged in cross-cultural conversations will affirm. Dialogue is transformative only to the extent that each partner is respected and given space to be fully oneself. In the same way, we learn most in dialogue with scripture when we are honest about our questions and even our objections.

This dialogical approach to scripture means that, with biblical scholar Elisabeth Schüssler Fiorenza, we regard scripture as prototype, not archetype.[12] To look at scripture as archetype means seeking to govern life by its every detail, uncritically examined, while silencing questions and experience. To look at scripture as prototype means approaching it as a key source for theological and ethical understandings that are always in process of development, as Schüssler Fiorenza writes:

> [Scripture] is the dynamic multifaceted root-model of Christian faith and practice. As such it does not need to be repeated but to be explored and transformed in order to open up a way into the future. Yet while the scope and dimensions of the Christian historical trajectory are open-ended, its direction and impulse is bound to its New Testament beginnings.[13]

Thus the church continues in dialogue with scripture, not as an authority to be obeyed, but as a wellspring for continuing growth in Christian faith and practice as God's presence is revealed in life and community. The church values both scripture and contemporary experience as arenas for God's presence and self-revelation. Just as Christians may challenge certain scripture passages based on their search for justice, peace, healing, and reconciliation, so scripture may challenge the church to move further along the road to these same four goals.

The imagination, informed by disciplined biblical study, keeps the words, images, and narratives of scripture in dialogue with human experience. Imagination brings new vitality to worship and faith, as United Church of Christ pastors William Abernethy and Philip Joseph Mayher argue: "Allowing images to come forth from the collective wellsprings of biblical tradition, as well as from our more personal sources, is to revive faith, to freshen conscious faith by baptism in its source waters."[14] Through imagination, women's experiences complement and at times correct the experience of men remembered in scripture, canon, and lectionary. Accustomed ways of perceiving the world may imprison our imaginations, but creative dialogue with scripture can free them.[15] Erik Routley has named the process of putting scripture into creative dialogue with human experience "scriptural resonance."[16] In Routley's opinion, hymn texts such as Scottish psalm paraphrases that simply quote scripture metrically do not help congregations gain access to scripture. Texts that draw only on human experience may serve one time or place, but they may not speak beyond a given year or community. When scripture reverberates in the sound box of human experience, worship empowers our faith and living.

Marjorie Procter-Smith, professor of worship, has written of the movement to restore biblical allusions, words, and images to worship.[17] New liturgies often use scripture typologically: They draw on repeated patterns in human experience or between the two testaments to make meaning. For example, baptismal liturgies highlight water symbolism by alluding to scriptures about the flood, the exodus, and the baptism of Jesus. Such images and metaphors illumine worship more than do the doctrinal propositions all too prevalent in earlier Protestant liturgies.

Keeping scripture central in worship—in dialogue with contemporary experience—is, for me, an important part of renewing the church. Scripture witnesses to God's love and call to humanity throughout time, and particularly in Jesus Christ; it holds together the challenge and grace of Christian living. Worship that is not scripturally grounded tends to depend too much on the concerns of particular pastoral leaders; keeping scripture central tends to nurture congregations in God's grace and challenge them by God's call. Worship with scriptural resonance connects a community with its heritage and with the larger church. Worship that honors both scripture and contemporary experience equips the whole people of God (clergy and laity) for ministry in the world. Further, since scripture often deals honestly and deeply with the realities of human life; its narratives and images can help modern people name their own realities. For all these reasons, scripture enriches Christian worship and provides its integrating focus.

Selecting and using scriptural ideas and images calls for good judgment, of course. Procter-Smith criticizes unreflective use of patriarchally charged images from scripture, such as those that use "Adam . . . as a type of all humanity" and Eve as a "type of sinful womanhood, or sometimes sinful humanity."[18] She argues for the need for imagination in worship, and she describes how women first become aware of the patterns of liberation and oppression in their lives and then "discover the same patterns in biblical narrative."[19] For example, Phyllis Trible has drawn imaginative connections between the woman in search of a lost coin and women searching "for something of value in a tradition that has devalued them."[20] Christine Smith in her book *Weaving the Sermon: Preaching in a Feminist Perspective* also speaks of women's imaginative and poetic use of scripture to speak to the experiences of worshiping communities.[21]

Through imagination, women articulate their experiences and bring them into dialogue with scripture texts. In this way, they assume their roles as interpreters-in-community of Christian tradition.

Summary

The creative, prophetic, judicious use of words contributes to the renewal of worship, when combined with attention to participation through senses, silence, and spontaneity. Silenced voices sound and the Christian witness speaks directly to local contexts and particular occasions. The words of scripture resound in dialogue with contemporary experiences. To find words for worship, we need the help of the Spirit, for we do not know how to pray as we ought (Rom. 8:26). God is greater than any human words, yet certain methods and disciplines—which we will explore in this book—can assist us in finding words to worship the God of Jesus Christ.

2

The Creative Process

Creativity is an important dimension of worship; and the creativity that best serves worship is a process, not a product. The creative process, which I will explore in this chapter, follows an interior structure or flow. It involves several steps, though the experienced creative person may pass through some steps very quickly or go back and forth between steps, not always in the same order. Anyone who becomes blocked in the process of preparing services, prayers, or sermons may benefit by following the steps I will describe.

The creative process is a bridge between right and left brain functions, between creativity and discipline. Right brain creative functions allow images, narratives, and feelings to surface that make worship services interesting. Left brain discipline allows us to choose among various imaginative possibilities and arrange ideas and images in an intelligible framework. The ability to move freely back and forth across the bridge that connects creativity and discipline, right and left brain, is essential for effective communication in worship.

Peter Elbow, author of *Writing with Power,* says that only exceptional people naturally find a balance between creativity and discipline in their writing:

> Ordinary writers fall into two camps. Either creativity has won out and produced writers who are rich but undisciplined, who can turn out lots of stuff with good bits in it, but who are poor at evaluating, pruning, and shaping. Or else critical thinking has won out and produced writers who are careful but cramped. They have great difficulty

> writing because they see faults in everything as they are trying to put
> it down on paper. . . . [Their writing] lacks the brilliance or excite-
> ment that comes from unhampered creativity.[1]

Elbow's evaluation describes my experience of editing books of
prayers. One sort of prayer-writer has several brilliant ideas and images buried in excess verbiage. Another is perfectly correct but
writes nothing to touch feeling or imagination. The best writers can
work with one basic idea or image and develop it clearly in a way
that touches people's hearts and makes them think.

The creative process is, of course by no means exclusive to
Christians. In fact, Christians often fear discipline (as if the Spirit
worked only through spontaneity) or creativity (as if Christians of
past generations had said everything worth saying). Although creativity is a human, not just a Christian activity, designing worship is
an expression of Christian faith. Thus, in describing the creative
process I draw on resources of Christian faith.

Step One: Beginning with Prayer

The first step in creative preparation for Christian worship is prayer,
or a prayerful attitude. Silent contemplation, meditative movement,
or a prayer spoken for inspiration can lead to a prayerful state, as
can playing a musical instrument or listening to music.

Etty Hillesum, who chronicled her experiences as a young
Jewish woman in the Netherlands from 1941 to 1943, spoke of
prayer in this way:

> There is a really deep well inside me. And in it dwells God. Sometimes
> I am there too. But more often stones and grit block the well, and God
> is buried beneath. Then [God] must be dug out again.
>
> I imagine that there are people who pray with their eyes turned heav-
> enwards. They seek God outside themselves. And there are those who
> bow their head and bury it in their hands. I think that these seek God
> inside.[2]

We can also seek God in the creative process of preparing to preach
or preparing words to help worshipers pray or sing God's praise.
The Spirit teaches us how to pray (Rom. 8:26; John 14:26). To be

open to the Spirit in the creative process means doing whatever it takes to remove the mud and the sticks so that the well of God's creative power springs up to guide our efforts.

Step Two: Engaging the Imagination

The second step of the creative process is to engage specific content through sense and experience, through your imagination. Perhaps you are working with a particular scripture passage as the focus of a service and sermon. If it is a narrative passage, picture yourself there. What do you see, hear, smell, taste, touch? Imagine yourself as a character in the story or the parable. What do you say or do? Try to sense the human dynamics at work in a passage from the epistles or the prophets. What is your entry point, experientially, into the text? What questions arise? What experiences does it bring to mind?[3]

Some people prefer to complete their exegetical work before entering into a text imaginatively. Exegesis can identify the context that gave rise to the questions the text addresses, thus uncovering narrative possibilities. Other people need to engage the text personally before reading what scholars have said, so that the text speaks for itself without the filter of the "experts." Each of us must evaluate for ourselves whether we most effectively begin with exegesis or contemplation of a text. Preparing responsibly to lead worship or preach involves both engaging a text personally *and* gaining scholars' perspectives. Exegesis highlights things that we might easily miss, suggesting intriguing new possibilities or helping us avoid misreading a text. Engaging a text through imagination and experience complements close exegetical study.

Perhaps your service focuses on a particular human need, for example, the theme may be homelessness. Then engage sense and experience related to homeless people. Recall a particular face or recall a street in your town where those who are homeless congregate. Or remember an experience in which you were uprooted, without a home. Imagine what it would be like for everyone to have a home. What would that look like, sound like, feel like?

Engaging the imagination enlivens the worship service, whether our focus is a scripture text or a human situation. The late biblical scholar Amos Wilder called for a rebirth of imagination in the life of the church:

> Imagination is a necessary component of all profound knowing and celebration; all remembering, realizing, and anticipating; all faith, hope, and love. When imagination fails doctrines become ossified, witness and proclamation wooden, doxologies and litanies empty, consolations hollow, and ethics legalistic.[4]

Imagination renews the church through image, myth, and symbol, reconnecting the biblical witness with the realities of human life. Wilder goes on to say that we cannot account for "the full mystery of language where deep calls to deep. . . . Any fresh renewal of language or rebirth of images arises from within and from beyond our control. Nevertheless we can help prepare the event."[5] Taking time to let the images of scripture and daily life speak prepares the way toward renewing the language of worship. Only through imagination can worship support spiritual formation and motivate persons to act on their Christian commitment in the world.

Step Three: Brainstorming

Our imaginations engaged, we can move to the third step of the creative process, often called brainstorming. In this step, we gather options for developing our work, without yet evaluating or choosing between them. Many methods of brainstorming exist. "Clustering," an excellent approach developed by Gabriele Rico, a professor of English and creative arts, begins with a word or phrase written in the center of a blank sheet of paper.[6] The word or phrase is like the trunk of a grapevine, and each branch is a "cluster" of related thoughts. Take, for example, the word "summer." One branch might develop words about vacations, another about hot weather, and another about summer sports. Clustering helps us imagine a variety of ways to develop a given theme.

A similar method was developed by composition teacher Rebecca Ferguson. The student "brainstorms" possible ideas for a theme, writing each idea on a separate small piece of paper, then gathering the slips of paper into groups of related ideas. Slips of paper with ideas that end up being extraneous are discarded.[7]

Group brainstorming generates many ideas, even if development of ideas is done individually, because one person's creativity
inspires that of another.

Brainstorming (however named or done) is an important part
of creative worship and sermon preparation. In the rush of parish
life, church leaders may too easily seize the first idea that presents
itself. This can result in too many services with similar themes and
not enough fresh ideas.

Step Four: Focusing

Some of us are very good at brainstorming but not as good at the
next step of the creative process: focusing. Creative work without
focus is like a garden overgrown with so many plants that no one
plant can grow to its fullness. A confused tangle replaces the beauty
of individual plants or the whole garden.

We all have heard sermons that have many engaging ideas and
narratives yet leave us wondering, "What was that about?" Few of
us have escaped hearing prayers that seem to wander aimlessly from
topic to topic, pious but lacking wings to carry us to the heart of
prayer. These experiences happen because the worship leader or
preacher did not focus thoughts around a theme or an orderly progression of themes. Many good sermons can be preached from the
same scripture text—but not all should be preached in one service!
Hymns, prayers, and sermons with a common focus help congregations move along with the flow of worship and thus to participate
more fully.

Sometimes the focus will leap out during the process of brainstorming; one idea or image will be more interesting than all the
others. The trunk/branch method of brainstorming is designed to let
a focus emerge naturally as the writer notices themes and images
common to various clusters or finds one cluster of ideas to be more
exciting than the others.[8]

At other times, a writer will need to make a conscious decision
between possible ideas. Here are some good reasons to choose one
idea over another, or to evaluate a focus tentatively chosen:

1. The focus addresses known needs of the congregation or particular members.
2. The focus provides a new angle on considering this passage of scripture or human experience.
3. The focus holds interesting possibilities for development through varied art forms. (For example, an image may suggest itself that can inspire a banner or liturgical movement, or resonate with a hymn the congregation loves well.)
4. The focus moves us into the heart of the gospel, keeping our minds on what is most important.
5. The focus challenges us to deal with issues we might otherwise avoid.

The first four reasons speak for themselves; the fifth may bear comment. After fifteen years of preaching and leading worship, I have finally discovered that I do some of my best work when I engage a difficult issue. Working with a difficult text or human situation is like Jacob's wrestling match with the angel: it calls on all our resources. We cannot rest until we have received a blessing—because, in the end, we must have something to say on Sunday. For example, after avoiding a passage from Hebrews about the blood of Jesus for four lectionary cycles, I chose it as the text for a chapel service and sermon. I researched the book of Hebrews and reflected freshly on the meaning of Jesus' death. I struggled through to a sermon through which God changed at least one life; I interpreted Jesus' sacrifice not as a model for human sacrifice of ourselves and others but as the end of sacrifice as the victimization of some humans by others. The Spirit used that word to help someone leave a situation where she was being sexually harassed. This might not have happened had I avoided the passage for the fifth time. Focusing on a challenging text or issue may call forth our best work, as this experience did for me.

Step Five: Letting Words Flow

For whatever reason, a focus has been chosen. The next step is to let ideas flow freely out of the brainstorming and focusing process. Many people are so anxious about their writing that they are unable to turn off their critical minds long enough to develop a first draft. Worries about grammar or the material's worth distract from getting ideas on paper. Turn off your inner censor at this stage of the process to give your imagination room to bring forth material worth editing.[9]

Methods for letting ideas flow differ from person to person. Some prefer to write longhand and others opt for a computer. Those who communicate more readily in oral than written forms may find it helpful to speak the first draft into a tape recorder. If all else fails, a friend can interview the blocked writer, taking copious notes to start the process of putting ideas into writing.

This fifth step—letting ideas flow freely—is essential to good writing. Neglecting it may engender prayers, sermons, or worship orders that are correct (grammatically or canonically) but not very interesting. The next two steps are just as important to refine our creativity. They involve leaving work alone for a while (step six), and returning to revise the work where needed (step seven).

Step Six: Taking Time Away

Most people who prepare sermons and worship orders do so in the midst of a busy life—between hospital calls and meetings, after work, or after the children have gone to sleep. The pressure of time makes it attractive to prepare worship at one sitting, yet time away allows us to be critical of our creative efforts. Each word, when freshly written, seems essential. Later, we can sharpen what is unclear and prune what is unnecessary. At least a day's distance from the material is best.

If this is impossible, then taking a break—moving physically away from the material and turning one's attention to something else for a while—helps. Distance from the material also can help us solve problems that stumped us at first. Time away is essential to discover and refine the best ideas possible.

Step Seven: Revising

When we have taken some time away, we are ready for the next step: revising and evaluating. I will devote the next chapter to the disciplines of using language in worship. Here I will simply address the importance of the discipline of revising. Without creative ideas, there is nothing worth revising, but without revising, there is nothing worth sharing.

The purpose of revising is to refine our spontaneous outpourings into words that will speak to others and not just to ourselves. We edit hymns, prayers, or sermons not to demonstrate our eloquence but to remove barriers to others' understanding and participation. An awkward rhyme in a hymn will distract the singer, who wonders, "Why in the world is this word here and what does the author mean? Oh, I see—'roll' is there to rhyme with 'soul'." A more fitting rhyme would not distract the singer from praise or prayer. Or a preacher will discard a sermon illustration that does not quite fit, because it might confuse the hearer. Or an image that more easily allows the worshiper to identify with the words of a prayer replaces an abstract idea or multisyllabic word. Revising, then, is important for the sake of communication, understanding, and involvement. Successful revising may require much more time than the initial writing, yet it makes our work worth sharing.

Revising requires humility and open-mindedness. Persons who are too attached to their writing to revise it are unlikely to develop polished communication that will engage others. Two novice hymn writers I knew were corresponding with an editor reviewing hymns for publication. One writer was very attached to the words she had written. She defended against changes on theological and poetic grounds, seemingly offended that the hymn could not be accepted as written. The other writer accepted suggestions eagerly. The reviewer asked her to work further on word choice, especially rhymes. The writer read each suggestion carefully, and she found a better solution every time. Neither hymn was finally accepted; early efforts at hymn writing are rarely published. The first hymn writer may have a greater natural gift of imagination, but the second writer—the one who was able to learn from constructive criticism—may well develop her gifts more fully than the other and be able to publish some day.

Step Eight: Learning from Feedback

A writer willing to revise is also able to follow step eight of the creative process: learning from feedback. Some people are so enamored of their own work that they cannot identify its weaknesses; others are so unsure of themselves that they fear feedback would discourage their creative work. Either way, they may avoid seeking feedback without which they will never fully develop their work. Feedback can help us identify words or ideas we use too frequently or words that may lead to misunderstandings of what we have written.

People with more talent and skill than we have can challenge us to greater precision or more beautiful form; members of a congregation can report whether and how our words touch their experience. If we want to grow, we must seek regular feedback from people whom we lead in worship and from colleagues whose work we respect and whom we can trust to be honest yet gentle with us and our work.

Hymn text writer Brian Wren speaks appreciatively of Erik Routley, one of the great scholars of hymnody in the twentieth century, who "demolished a feeble (and lengthy) hymn" Wren had sent him, but encouraged him to keep writing.[10] W. Thomas Smith notes that Routley later called Wren "the most successful English hymn writer since Charles Wesley."[11] Wren's experience reminds us that even the finest writers do not begin with polished skills; learning from feedback can help them be the best writers they can be.

Summary

The creative process takes many forms. Editing a hymn text, a dance, or a banner design involves different issues. At times an idea emerges in a rough form that will require extensive work; at other times, ideas come forth almost fully formed and the process of brainstorming, focusing, and editing takes much less time.

A systematic understanding of the creative process can help us identify what parts of the process we are shortchanging. For example, learning more about the creative process caused me to realize that I neglect brainstorming while designing a sermon; I sometimes focus too quickly and miss the best ideas. My work in editing worship and hymn resources makes it abundantly clear to me that many writers do not spend enough time revising their work. Others neglect the step of getting in touch with sense and experience; their work is polished but unimaginative.

Although the creative process takes many forms, it has an inner structure with identifiable parts that can be neglected only at the risk of impoverishing our work. Considering the creative process can help us break through problems in finishing a project, perhaps by engaging our imaginations or brainstorming new approaches. Most of all, reflection on the creative process reveals what hard work and commitment it takes to find words for worship. Only our best efforts, guided by the Spirit at work in us and our congregations, are worthy of the goal of helping congregations express their heartfelt prayer and praise to God.

3

Disciplines of Writing for Worship

Finding words for a congregation's prayer and praise calls for strenuous discipline as well as creativity. Worship should include unrehearsed, spontaneous elements; yet the written parts of worship deserve careful editing. A garden needs weeding if it is to be beautiful; a song needs practice before it is sung before others; and words for worship need editing before people speak them. In this chapter, I explore the varied disciplines involved in writing for worship.

Special Characteristics of
Liturgical Writing

Words for worship have special requirements, since they differ both from literary prose and poetry and from informal speech. The language of worship is oral; it is meant to be spoken. Unlike a theological treatise or a poem, words of worship must be accessible on first hearing. This calls for simple and direct words and sentences. Yet the language of worship is not identical to that of everyday speech. Paying attention to the sound of words can lead to an engaging euphony, and attention to rhythm can help people speak together. Further, words for worship are not simply the expression of an individual person; they must be something the whole congregation can say honestly. Let us then consider the particular disciplines of finding words for worship.

Common Voice

Words spoken in worship are more than the creative expression of one individual; they speak for an entire worshiping community in its diversity. Paradoxically, words spoken honestly from the deep places of an individual heart may resonate deeply with others' experiences.

Yet one pitfall in speaking from the creative voice in worship is that, given people's different life experiences and spiritual journeys within a congregation, one person's honest expression may be irrelevant or even alienating to another. One way to avoid this pitfall is to involve varied persons, lay and clergy, in developing a congregation's worship. Anyone developing words for worship could benefit from Fred Craddock's advice to preachers. He asks preachers to envision the congregation while preparing a sermon:

> Who will hear the sermon? No general answer is satisfactory; close your eyes and see the people in the pews. They can be seen clearly because they sit in the same places every week. Let the names of the listeners come to mind and be formed by the lips.[1]

Envisioning the congregation—and its individual members— helps leaders be faithful in speaking to them, even when bringing the gospel challenge to accustomed ways of living. Thinking of a particular worshiping community can help writers avoid individual idiosyncrasies and find a common voice, even when writing for a general audience. The goal is not to impose one's beliefs and experiences but to walk alongside other Christians, giving voice to shared experiences and challenges of life and faith.

Giving voice to shared experiences implies honesty in naming the nature of living as a Christian in a particular time and place. Such honesty calls those of us who prepare words for worship to listen closely to ourselves and to the people with whom we share the journey of faith. Then, in prayer, we voice those things that seem to be shared in community. At times we may risk speaking from our own experience even if it does not seem to be shared by all. Speaking in moderation from our own experience can be helpful, for we may put into words what is yet inarticulate in others. Speaking too much from our own experience may mean, however, that we are not listening and are overemphasizing experiences not shared by all.

"Speaking the truth in love" (Ephesians 4:15a) is the byword for honesty in finding words for worship. "Speaking the truth" means that our prayer touches down into daily experience; "in love" means not simply speaking for ourselves, but seeking to voice the concerns of a worshiping community.

One way to support the common voice is to use first-person plural pronouns such as "we" and "our," though this is not always necessary. During the 1970s and 1980s, church leaders altered hymn texts to emphasize the communal nature of the church. The Presbyterian hymnal of 1972 aimed at diminishing "excessive introspective use of first person singular pronouns"; for example, "I love your kingdom, Lord" was changed to "We love your kingdom, Lord".[2] On the other hand, some churches changed the popular chorus to sing, "Spirit of the living God, fall afresh on *us*," when, perhaps, individual openness to the Spirit is the issue at stake. It is more commonly recognized today that "I," when sung together in community, often implies a communal consciousness. For example, church music in the African American tradition often uses "I," meant communally, reflecting the African proverb: "I am, because we are." At the same time, using "we" and "us" may be better in some churches that appear to be overly individualistic in their approach to Christian faith.

Awareness of One's Audience

Awareness of one's audience, important in every kind of writing, is an acute issue in writing for worship. We must be aware of whether we are addressing God or human beings in each part of the service. We also must be sensitive to the concerns and language patterns of the congregations who will be experiencing these words in worship. Because words are never adequate to address the living God, we approach the task of shaping words for worship with reverence and humility.

Annie Dillard has written of walking across a slope planted in apple trees to buy communion wine. She asked herself, "Who am I to buy the communion wine? . . . Shouldn't I be wearing robes and, especially, a mask? Shouldn't I *make* the communion wine? Are there holy grapes, is there holy ground, is anything here holy?"[3] She concludes that "there are no holy grapes, there is no holy ground, nor is there anyone but us" to send.[4] Dillard highlights here the rather astonishing reality that mere humans count ourselves worthy to design worship, write prayers, or prepare for communion. Some seem almost careless in their worship, as if unaware they are addressing the living God. Yet Dillard suggests that it is foolhardy to think that even the most carefully designed liturgy is truly worthy to worship the holy God:

> The higher Christian churches—where, if anywhere, I belong—come at God with an unwarranted air of professionalism, with authority and pomp, as though they knew what they were doing, as though people in themselves were an appropriate set of creatures to have dealings with God. I often think of the set pieces of liturgy as certain words which people have successfully addressed to God without their getting killed. . . . If God were to blast such a service to bits, the congregation would be, I believe, genuinely shocked. But in the low churches you expect it any minute. This is the beginning of wisdom.[5]

This wry observation about styles of worship points to two dangers of preparing words for worship. Some of us may so value spontaneity and informality that we are careless of our words and actions, fostering a breezy intimacy that is not worthy of God's worship. Others of us may take our words too seriously, as if a technology of correct words and forms could assure proper approach to God. Then our stuffy reverence may not help people open their lives to God.

Søren Kierkegaard, the Danish theologian, is often quoted as saying that God is the audience and the congregation is the actor in worship.[6] This was his alternative to an assumption he rightly criticized—the assumption that in worship clergy are the actors, God is the prompter, and the congregation is the audience. But the idea that God is the audience in worship is one-sided and too narrow. God both speaks and hears in Christian worship; God, as well as human participants, acts in worship. At heart, Christian worship concerns the relationship between God and humans. This is not precisely a theology of partnership, since God's love, power, and wisdom exceed ours. A relational understanding of worship makes room for reverence and for intimacy, since this loving, powerful, and wise God seeks to be in a covenant relationship with us. An appropriate theology of worship, then, calls for language reflecting reverent intimacy.

The language that reflects reverent intimacy depends on cultural context. Reverent intimacy is, I believe, expressed most appropriately through the best of everyday language. In the working-class and middle-class congregations in which I have ministered, churches made up of mostly middle-aged to older German or English Americans, that has meant avoiding slang, abstraction, and extreme formality while attending to correct grammar. Prayers I have written for these congregations might seem too pedestrian to a highly educated upper-class congregation or too formal to a congregation of teenagers or young adults. Furthermore, reverent intimacy comes more from attitude than from words. I have worshiped with a charismatic Puerto Rican Disciples of Christ congregation that was extremely informal in its style, yet who expressed a joyful sense of awe and love toward the God of love and power.

Few congregations are uniform in their educational levels or ethnic backgrounds. Many include some people whose first language is not the one used in worship. This demands simple, direct, and pictorial language that, fortunately, characterizes good writing in general. Writer George Orwell praised the powerful words of Ecclesiastes 9:11, given here in the NRSV translation:

> Again I saw that under the sun the race is not to the swift, nor the battle to the strong, nor bread to the wise, nor riches to the intelligent, nor favor to the skillful; but time and chance happen to them all.

By contrast, he said, people today tend to use multisyllabic, abstract words and jargon to obscure truth or to pretend scientific impartiality. Orwell parodied modern writers as they might express the thought in Ecclesiastes:

> Objective consideration of contemporary phenomena compels the conclusion that success or failure in competitive activities exhibits no tendency to be commensurate with innate capacity, but that a considerable element of the unpredictable must invariably be taken into account.[7]

The scripture passage uses forty-four words, fifty-three syllables, and six vivid images. Orwell's parody uses thirty-eight words, ninety syllables, and no images.[8] He urged writers to avoid long, abstract words and to find concrete images to express their ideas. Imagery is so important in the language of worship that I will devote chapter 4 to the topic.

Unison prayers and hymn texts call for common rhythms and words of mostly one or two syllables. People need common rhythms and words in order to speak together. Consider the simple rhythms that characterize high school cheers or chants at peace demonstrations. The high school cheer, "Spirit! Let's hear it! Jump! Shout! Let it out!" wouldn't be the same if we said, "Manifest your enthusiasm."[9] We cry not "Eliminate nuclear proliferation!" but rather "No more weapons; give us peace!" People with sophisticated theological training may prefer the precision of long, abstract words, but such words will not help congregations pray. Good phrasing also calls for careful rhythm. The rhythm of "We have followed too much the devices and desires of our own hearts"[10] surpasses the rhythm of "The direction for our perambulations is provided by our defense mechanisms and libidinal urges." The tongue can test whether rhythm is graceful; the unison prayer, an oral form, is best tested orally. The rhythm of unison speech sometimes resembles the rhythmic patterns of poetic speech. For example, in the phrase "No more weapons; give us peace," every other syllable is stressed. Rhythms for unison prayer are more subtle and complex than that, but using words of few syllables, saying prayers aloud, and then editing them can help people speak in unison.

Because worship addresses our relationship with God, it speaks in the language of the heart, which is clear and direct, rather than in abstraction and excess verbiage. Direct prayer language calls for active verbs ("you have led us"), more than passive verbs ("we are led by you"). Compare the example above, "We have followed the devices and desires of our hearts," with "The direction for our perambulations is provided by our defense mechanisms and libidinal urges." "We have followed" uses an active verb form; "the direction for our perambulations is provided by" uses a passive verb form ("is provided"), combined with a complicated construction using two abstract nouns.

Although, like Orwell, I have parodied bad writing in its extreme form, such passive, complicated constructions abound in locally created liturgies. Good liturgical writing uses simple words and constructions.

Address

Some prayers begin by speaking *to* God, then slip into speaking *about* God, as do the following words: "We thank you, God, for coming to us in Jesus Christ, who shows us the ways of God." To say ". . . who came to show us your ways" would be more consistent. Consistently speaking to God in prayer helps worshipers direct their attention to God. Worship leaders should also resist the temptation to use prayers to persuade or educate the congregation. Corporate prayer is not the time for explanations. Consider the prayer: "We come to you on this day of Epiphany, which celebrates the manifestation of Christ to the Gentiles." Obviously, God already knows the meaning of Epiphany; the worship leader is furtively inserting an explanation, in case anyone in the congregation did not know. A prayer after preaching is not the place for sermon summaries; it is an opportunity to voice common prayer in response to scripture reading and sermon. A prayer of confession is not the time to express only one side of a controversial issue. For example, I could honestly pray in private: "Forgive our country for waging war on Iraq." Yet if I spoke the same words while leading worship, some of the congregation might suspect that I was trying to change their minds about a controversial issue. When a prayer includes more than one sentence that does not directly address God with "you" or "your," preaching or teaching has probably replaced praying. Careful editing can help, but the best way to avoid such problems is to turn our minds toward God in prayer even when writing a prayer.

Always remember to whom you are speaking. At times worship leaders shift abruptly into prayer *to* God in a part of worship when they have been speaking *about* God. Admittedly, we can find examples to support this in the language of the psalms. Psalm 104 begins and ends by addressing the soul: "Bless the LORD, O my soul." Then, verses 1–30 speak directly to God: "You are clothed with honor and majesty. . . ." In verse 31 the psalm shifts to talking about God in the third person: "May the glory of the LORD endure forever." Even the psalms, however, generally make a shift in person in a logical way, with one section addressing God and another addressing the people. A call to worship or greeting may do the same thing, first naming God's deeds to the congregation, then inviting worshipers to join in praise, then addressing God. Unannounced shifts should have a similar internal logic. With the exception of greetings or calls to worship modeled on the psalms, it is better to address either God or the congregation rather than to shift back and forth without such cues as "Let us pray."

Common Linguistic Problems

Paying careful attention to the grammar appropriate to the culture and language of worshipers is a part of using the best of human language to speak to the living God. Some church leaders may want to study books on grammar and composition.[11] Here I mention only the difficulties that most commonly appear in words written for worship by local church leaders.

Economy of Language

The most important linguistic discipline in preparing words for worship is economy of language. Anything extraneous to the focus of a sermon, hymn, or prayer is best deleted. Repetition should be used only to build rhythm or intensity. Martin Luther King Jr.'s repeated words "I have a dream" built both. Using synonyms such as "hate and hostility" in a prayer of confession, however, is merely repetitive. Every word should contribute to the forward movement of thoughts and feelings.

Consistency

One should be consistent—at least in a given prayer or hymn, if not a whole service—in using forms such as "thee" or "you." Most people are not aware of all the complexities of language based on the King James Version of the Bible, and they would do better to use contemporary forms. To say the least, a prayer such as "O God, we give *thee* thanks for all *you* have done for us" is inconsistent and needs editing. Similarly, those who prepare printed resources for worship should avoid inconsistency about capitalizing pronouns for

God, as in this example: "We give *You* thanks for all *you* do." Most books of worship and hymnals today tend not to capitalize pronouns for God, except, of course, at the beginning of sentences. Either practice is acceptable, if observed consistently.

Theological consistency is harder to measure, but some examples may point in the right direction. Anyone who considers the Holy Spirit to be a personal reality will want to avoid using "it" in reference to the Spirit. Any who affirm that Jesus the Christ is truly human and truly divine will want to avoid calling Jesus a "creature of God," which implies that Jesus is only human, not God. Complete theological consistency would probably require silencing many voices within a denomination or congregation. Yet preparing words for worship requires theological care so that the words reach toward saying what the congregation truly means.

"O" and "Oh"

"O" and "oh" have different meanings. "O" precedes a name, as a formal or poetic address.[12] "Oh" is used to express surprise or to attract someone's attention.[13] I believe some persons begin a prayer "Oh, God . . ." because "O" seems archaic or overly formal; but using "oh" means either we need to attract God's attention or we are expressing a chummy familiarity. A better alternative would be to recast the prayer in order to avoid using "O," as many contemporary prayers do.

Punctuation

Although punctuation may seem like a minor matter, it can be crucial in preparing words for worship. Properly placed commas in unison prayers or hymns alert a congregation when to breathe. Further, in worship, we do not have the luxury of experiencing words several times until we understand them. Punctuation (written or given through appropriate pauses in speaking) helps people understand the words the first time. For example, a prayer began, "According to the witness of David, Isaiah, and John the Messiah was coming to free the people of Israel." A comma after "John" would have saved me a few moments of wondering who "John the Messiah" was. Correct punctuation helps people understand and speak a prayer.

Prayers that are written locally often incorrectly punctuate direct address of God or humanity. When someone is directly addressed in the middle of a sentence, commas are placed both at the beginning and the end: "We thank you, God, for all you do for us." Address at the beginning or end of a sentence is set off by one comma: "O God, we thank you." "We thank you, O God."

Grammar

Written prayers should almost always be complete sentences, though incomplete sentences can be effective in sermons or prayers spoken by one voice.[14] Written prayers should be punctuated properly. Incorrect use of commas, semicolons, or periods can make it difficult for a congregation to determine where a thought begins and ends. A complete clause (with subject and verb) should be set off with a semicolon or period; joining two complete clauses with only a comma (technically called a "comma splice") causes confusion. Observing these basic guidelines of punctuation can help people understand a hymn or prayer more quickly.

Sense Lines

Laying out a prayer in "sense lines" helps people divide prayers into appropriate phrases. Through sense lines, each new thought unit begins a new line, even where punctuation is inappropriate. This blessing by Janet Morley paraphrases the apocryphal scripture Wisdom of Solomon 7:25–27, which uses "holy Wisdom" as an image for God. It demonstrates the use of sense lines:

> May holy Wisdom,
> kind to humanity,
> steadfast, sure and free,
> the breath of the power of God;
> may she who makes all things new, in every age,
> enter our souls,
> and make us friends of God,
> through Jesus Christ, Amen.[15]

Sense lines help individuals to read aloud smoothly and helps groups to stay together as they read and understand the meaning of a prayer more quickly.

Simplicity

While worshipers are singing or praying, there is no time for them to unravel complicated sentences. Short, simple sentences in printed worship materials help people understand. Simple sentence structure is crucial for anything received only in oral form since hearers cannot reread what they did not understand the first time. Simple sentences with no subordinate clauses are usually best, except when a repeated structure helps hearers follow: "When we are tired, when we are hopeless, when we despair, God walks beside us and helps us carry our load." Obviously, rules cannot ensure good oral communication. Ask yourself several questions as you write: Does this flow well? Will it be clear? How can I simplify the structure for easier speaking and understanding? Are there places where I stumble when I say these words aloud? Considering these questions will help you refine the words to be spoken in worship.

Proofreading

Remember, no one but you knows what you *meant* to say. You must proofread your work, lest it provide unplanned humor, like the bulletin bloopers that grace Martin Marty's column in *The Christian Century:*

> The Christian Church of Elmwood and Unadilla, Nebraska, in its call to worship asked Almighty God to "deliver us . . . from wondering of mind."
>
> Worshipers at Syracuse University Protestant Campus Ministry were asked to be distinctly non-Barthian in the opening hymn: "Joyful, Joyful, We Above Thee."[16]
>
> Hively Avenue Mennonite Church in Elkhart, Indiana, divides its services into parts: after "WE HEAR THE WORD FROM GOD" comes "WE HARE WITH EACH OTHER." Rabbit, run?[17]

Other typographical errors aren't even good for a chuckle; they simply distract people from prayer.

Words for worship can be correct but also lifeless. The point of your writing should not be linguistic perfection, but clear communication. By addressing the issues raised in this section you can help congregations follow along more easily, rather than stumbling over what is unclear or grammatically incorrect, thereby making worship more immediately rewarding.

Inclusive Language

The African American spiritual, "Woke Up This Morning," expresses the inclusiveness of the gospel:

> Woke up this morning with my mind, and it was stayed, stayed on Jesus. Hallelu!
> Can't hate your neighbor in your mind, if you keep it stayed, stayed on Jesus. Hallelu!
> Makes you love everybody with your mind, when you keep it stayed, stayed on Jesus. Hallelu![18]

Genuine relationship with Jesus Christ leads us away from hatred and toward love of all people, beyond the constraints of cultural prejudices. The good news of God's love in Christ is meant for all people; no one is excluded on the basis of economic status, ethnic heritage, or sex. Baptism has been called the sacrament of equality, supported by this passage from the apostle Paul: "As many of you as were baptized into Christ have clothed yourselves with Christ. There is no longer Jew or Greek, there is no longer slave or free, there is no longer male or female; for all of you are one in Christ Jesus" (Gal. 3:27–28).

The witness to the gospel must reflect, rather than undermine, the baptismal equality of Christians and must witness to the all-inclusive love of God who creates all people in the divine image. Thus, words for Christian worship should honor all people and demean no one. To honor all people means avoiding expressions that render women invisible and assume that men are the normative human beings. Thus, it means using terms such as "man," "men," or "brothers," only when speaking of specific males. To respect diverse humanity means avoiding images that reinforce prejudices about childhood, youth, and age, as well as images that identify blindness with sin and sight with salvation. Words that identify blackness with sin reinforce racial prejudices. Arthur Clyde, editor of the 1995 United Church of Christ hymnal, reported that an African American consultant to the committee studied the use of "dark" in a major hymnal and found that in all of the 131 uses of the word, the connotation was negative.[19] Such imagery is problematic in this society so plagued with racism against darker-skinned persons.

Keeping all these issues in mind is challenging and difficult. For example, the original text of the hymn "Holy, Holy, Holy" includes the following phrase: "Though the eye of sinful man thy glory may not see." This phrase implies that men and not women are sinful. An attempt to correct it in one hymnal was worded: "Though the eye made blind by sin thy glory may not see."[20] But this version seems to support the all-too-common idea that disabilities result from someone's sin. Solving one problem may create another. Diverse human needs call for patience with ourselves and others, rather than perfectionism that carps at every slight. Witness to the inclusiveness of the gospel means paying attention to each word used to speak about humanity. Although general guidelines may apply, inclusiveness is best worked out in community with input from everyone with concerns to share.

Summary

Those who find words for worship must exercise great care, humility, honesty, and compassion when speaking for their worshiping communities. Words for worship should nurture a congregation's relationship with God, speaking with as much theological integrity as possible. Simple words and phrases, good grammar, and inclusive language help people to worship. At their best, words for worship channel the imagination into disciplined, honest, and clear speech. Thus, through the working of the Spirit, words for worship lead people into the presence of God.

4

Finding Images for Worship

"Savior, like a shepherd lead us." "A mighty fortress is our God." "I am the vine, you are the branches." "The Spirit rested like tongues of flame on their heads." "We have wandered from your way like lost sheep." "When I was a child, I was exhilarated by swinging on a swing placed high above a waterfall. It was risky, but breathtakingly beautiful. Taking risks on faith can be like that." Hymns, scripture readings, prayers, and sermons are full of imagery—sense impressions that keep the language of faith vivid.[1]

The Importance of Imagery

Imagery is central to the creative voice in worship. Concrete imagery holds people's interest more than abstract concepts do; it balances the simple, pared-down quality of good liturgical writing. The short, simple sentences and words that worship requires can easily become boring or trite without images on which we can focus. The expression of deep human feelings may bring a prayer to life, but appealing to the senses can keep feelings from seeming maudlin or romantic.

Although it engages our attention, imagery is more than a rhetorical device or ornament. Through imagery, ideas are embodied and given shape in terms of everyday reality. Imagery can engage the imagination so that worshipers do not simply think about what is said, but participate in it. The celebration of the Passover, for example, allows people to affirm that "we were slaves in Egypt" by recalling the narrative of the exodus, using vivid imagery and symbolism. In the process, children learn and adults affirm the story of a people not only as historical fact but as a narrative in which they participate. Imagination can make the past come alive.

Because imagery engages the imagination, it generates energy toward the future. Those engaged in healing ministry sometimes use guided imagery to picture the presence of Christ in human pain[2] or to visualize restored health,[3] for imagination releases healing energy. Similarly, while focusing on the immensity of the world's present problems immobilizes us, visualizing a world free from war and injustice mobilizes us to work for a better world.

Yet imagery also names present experience. In an opening prayer on an Easter Sunday, I thanked God for crocuses pushing up, trees budding, and birds flying north: all literal sense imagery. Then I gave thanks for Jesus Christ, who brings springtime to our souls and calls us out of the tombs of our apathy and despair. A church member later told me this expressed exactly how she was feeling. Vague statements about apathy and new life probably would not have named her experience, but vivid images from a world awakening to spring did.

Uses of Imagery in Worship

Worship uses imagery in several ways. At the beginning of the Easter prayer mentioned above, I used imagery literally to speak of the changing season. Then I spoke metaphorically, connecting renewal in Christ to the renewal of growing things in the spring.

Imagery can bring a narrative alive. Drawing on more than one sense in hymns, prayers, and sermons engages more people, given the fact that different people respond more fully to different senses. A preacher can help a congregation to imagine walking down the road to Emmaus, to see the faces of the two disciples who encountered the risen Christ, or to taste the broken bread (Luke 24:13–35). These sensory details go beyond what the text gives us, and they transport listeners to another time and place; through imagination we participate in the story. Thus the preacher helps the congregation experience Luke's point: Christ is among Christians when they break bread together.

Worship often employs metaphorical imagery to speak of God. A metaphor is a figure of speech that describes one reality in terms of another that is both like and unlike it. The expression "Necessity is the mother of invention" could be translated literally "When we desperately need to solve a problem, we come up with solutions we could not imagine otherwise." Necessity is not a child-bearing mammal, yet it does produce new ideas. Metaphors make meaning by speaking of one thing as if it were another, drawing us to understand by making connections we might not otherwise notice.

Worship draws on metaphors from daily life to describe God, who is present in our lives but transcends them, and who cannot be described fully through ordinary human language. For example, when Jesus called God "Father," he was using language metaphorically. Our relationship with God may resemble our relationship to a good and loving father, but God is not literally a human male; God's goodness and love is greater than that of the best father. (There is evidence in early Christian literature that Jesus also called God "Mother," as another way of describing our relationship with God.)[4] Even to speak of God as "love" is to use a metaphor based on human relationships. God is personal but not human; thus divine love, which encompasses all creation and never fails, is both like and unlike human love.

We use our best language—the language of everyday life and relationships—to speak of God, who is beyond our comprehension. We can speak of God as an animal—the lamb who was slain or the lion who defends her cubs. We can even call God a rock—not because God is inanimate, but because God is steadfast like a rock. Such images grasp toward that which cannot be fully put into words, yet must be expressed: living experience of the God who has come to humanity in Jesus Christ.

Metaphors enable us to speak of God in ways that open us to new insight. Metaphors such as "necessity is the mother of invention" and "Christ brings springtime to our souls" may be too familiar to engage our imaginations. Brian Wren's metaphor for God, "Carpenter of new creation," engages our sense of wonder, since God does not create with wood but with lives.[5]

Use of imagery, as sense description or metaphor, is based in a theology of incarnation. Episcopal priest and preaching professor Patricia Wilson-Kastner describes the incarnational nature of preaching:

> It tries through words to picture the activity of God in the matter of this world, its time and space, and all its human and animal inhabitants. Preaching focuses its words in the concrete, the specific, and the ordinary, because the God we know through the Bible became flesh for us in Jesus Christ.[6]

Like Jesus' parables from nature and household life, imagery in preaching, prayer, and hymns points to God's activity in daily life.

Christine Smith argues from a feminist perspective that using imagery from daily life in preaching and worship values the embodied reality of women and men where we find God loving and acting. Moreover, imagining a transformed future can inspire new, more just realities:

> For feminist women preachers in the Christian church, the use of the imagination is not an artistic luxury but a vital necessity in our work as weavers of the word. The imagination not only allows us to envision a future where justice is pervasive and our own marginality ceases to exist, but it also gives us the creative and persistent energy and hope to bring that kind of future into being.[7]

Use of imagery gives expression to life experiences of women and others that the church has silenced.

Reimaging Our Images of God

The current debate about gender and language for God provides an opportunity to become more creative in our use of imagery. A few images, such as Father, King, Lord, and Savior, have been used constantly in Christian worship for centuries. Because the church began and even now exists in societies that value men more highly than women, images for God have usually been male. Some languages do not use gendered pronouns, but English provides no third-person personal pronoun without gender, and in English, most pronouns used for God have been masculine. Grammar books of earlier centuries explicitly said that masculine pronouns were appropriate for God, who has no gender, because the male human is more valuable than the female.[8]

There are many good reasons to find ways of speaking about God that do not reflect cultural attitudes that value males over females. One reason is ethical. No serious theologian claims God is literally male. Constantly using male language for God, however, supports male dominance by (1) implying that men are more like God than women and (2) rendering women invisible by not mentioning them. Language that identifies a dominant group (e.g., males, masters, or parents) with God and makes others invisible or submissive (e.g., women, slaves, children) shapes the way we think. It makes it seem as if members of the more "godlike" group are worthy to control the others, even through coercion and violence. Jesus demonstrated mutual respect and not domination between males and females. Language that values men more than women is not consistent with a gospel ethic. The imagery of worship should provide alternatives to cultural values that do not reflect God's love and justice for all.

Using a broader range of imagery—including female imagery and pronouns for God along with more traditional imagery— witnesses to the Gospel more effectively. It demonstrates the all-inclusive love of God and opens new pathways to nurture relationship with God. Christians are free to use metaphors drawn from present human experience as well as from scripture and tradition, because of God's ongoing presence in human life, drawing from all people toward love, peace, and justice.

Most Christians are unaware of the rich diversity of metaphors for God in scripture and church tradition. A group of friends was discussing the much-debated use of Sophia language for God. One Roman Catholic was sympathetic but surprised. He said, "We would never speak of God that way in the Catholic church!" Someone responded by saying that God is called Sophia, the Greek word for wisdom, in apocryphal books that the Roman church considers canonical; she had heard one such passage read in the Easter vigil the night before. The first person responded, "But we never hear about it in church!" Exactly!

Familiar words of worship may seem to exhaust the possibilities of scriptural imagery for God, but they do not. For example, the God who seeks the lost is not only a loving father seeking a prodigal son but a woman seeking a lost coin (Luke 15:8–32). God is a fortress (Psalm 46:1, 11, NRSV footnote), and the rock who gave birth to Israel (Deut. 32:18). God, the fountain of life (Psalm 36:9), also has wings under which all people may take refuge (Psalm 36:7). The images for God in scripture, as well as those from Christian experience, are numerous.[9]

In leading classes and workshops about language for God, I find it helpful to begin by inviting people to share images of God from their personal prayer. This reminds participants that we are not discussing an abstract theological issue but are walking on the holy ground of people's relationship with God. People often mention images based on scripture, such as father, mother, Spirit, light, shepherd, and Lord. Others draw on images from nature as they seek to put into words their experience of God's presence: "like a flowing river" or "a cloud that surrounds me." Others compare their relationship with God to significant relationships with parents, friends, and lovers. My images of God have often centered around listening and hearing, so I am drawn to the image of God as a listening ear described by Nelle Morton, the late theological educator.[10] At other times, I might describe God as a bubbling joy and fiery energy within me. Images based on our contemporary experience should complement those from scripture and tradition so that worship and personal devotion are more closely connected in a congregation's worship.

Through imagery, creativity and discipline come together in our words for worship. Creativity is expressed largely through images; and the search for the most adequate images to worship the living God requires discipline. All of us have ways of speaking about God that we prefer through experience or habit. The challenge facing us as we lead communities in prayer is to speak genuinely out of our relationship with God, without over-emphasizing our favorite images. This involves intentionally expanding imagery to support all people in their lives of prayer and discipleship.

Patricia Wilson-Kastner suggests practicing several other disciplines in regard to imagery about God. She notes that to be effective, images must be familiar enough to call on worshipers' experience; they must be carefully chosen so that the worshiper's physical reality corresponds well to the invisible reality to which the image points.[11] Worship leaders also should select imagery for God that fits the context in worship. Some worship leaders customarily address every prayer to "Almighty God" or "Heavenly Father." The creative use of imagery in worship means searching for names that bring out a particular quality of God that is highlighted in a particular worship service. The scripture texts or themes for the day may suggest names for God; a service on Psalm 23 or John 10 might name God as shepherd, while a service focusing on the arts call God "creator" or even "creative artist of creation."

Imagery also must be vivid to be effective. An ancient image such as "shepherd" becomes more lively when the lives of shepherds and sheep are portrayed with detail and poignancy. "Springtime" was a vivid image one Easter only because the first signs of spring were erupting in Chicago that very week. The more specific and concrete an image, the more vivid it will be: "crocus" is more vivid than "flower," but naming a more unusual (but familiar) flower would have been more vivid still. Similarly, in the same hymn in which Brian Wren called God "Carpenter of new creation" and "Womb and Birth of time," he wrote, "God is love."[12] By coordinating the metaphor "love" with less common metaphors, Wren's naming of God becomes even more exciting and thought provoking. On the one hand, he makes newer and less familiar metaphors more acceptable by tying them to a familiar one; on the other, he brings new life to a very common metaphor by associating it with others.

Liturgical scholar Gail Ramshaw has rightly observed that while mixing metaphors is not desirable in ordinary language, liturgy can successfully pile up metaphors.[13] Some metaphors are so familiar that we forget they are metaphors; "Christ," for instance, means "anointed one." Metaphors for the divine can complement one another (as those in Wren's hymn do). They may also limit one another, as when the metaphors "rock" and "friend" describe God's faithfulness. God is personal, unlike a rock, yet steadfast and unchanging as a rock (more than any human friend) in befriending us.

One warning. Although using more than one metaphor may enhance communication in most services, one image should be central, with others coordinated around it. The metaphors, taken together, should support a unified focus in a service. Overusing one image will seem forced, while piling up too many images in one service will be confusing (unless the theme of the service is images of God). Thoughtful coordination of complementary images stimulates the imagination of worshipers.

Thoughtful use of imagery for worship means avoiding an imbalance of male imagery for God. Several strategies are possible. One strategy ("nonsexist language") is to lessen or avoid gender language in speaking about God. Another ("inclusive language") is to balance male and female imagery. The first strategy allows the use of some familiar terms, but limits the possibilities. The second adds new images without asking people to surrender the familiar. Yet it also can be problematic, if, for instance, all female images used for God are maternal, as if women are like God only when being mothers. Thus, language that honors both women and men is "emancipatory": it consciously portrays God at work on behalf of justice and dignity for the oppressed and marginalized.[14] Expanding our imagery for God requires careful awareness of images and the theology they imply.

Most discussions today about balancing imagery in worship focus on dealing carefully with human difference, such as gender or race, as we speak about God. Other kinds of balance also are worthy of theological reflection. For example, one church may tend to picture God as a distant, awe-inspiring ruler, while another usually speaks to God in the chummy, casual way one speaks to a close friend. Theologically, one could say that the first church emphasizes God's transcendence (magnificence, power, and holiness as compared to humanity), while the other emphasizes God's immanence (God's close presence in this world). More balanced imagery in each case, language that speaks both of God's greatness and God's closeness, would be preferred theologically.

Leading a congregation toward a broader range of imagery for God is not an abstract theological issue because it involves members' faith experience. A wise pastoral approach is to be gentle, gradual, dialogical, yet committed in your language. Forcing everyone to change their imagery by pastoral decree runs counter to the emphasis on justice and egalitarian values that inclusive language seeks to support. Failing to help congregations expand language is pastorally irresponsible, since expanded imagery for God nurtures spiritual life and a just society. Strategies for change differ with each context, but they should at least be characterized by mutual respect, honest sharing, and careful listening.

Carefully expanding our imagery for God is less a danger than an opportunity. A renewal of imagination in worship supports the renewal of the church and its mission. Overusing certain metaphors for God blunts their power to evoke wonder; it leads not to vital worship, vibrant spiritual life, or committed discipleship, but to stagnation. Vivid and varied imagery connects Christians today with the church's past journey with God, names present experience, and supports movement toward God's future of peace and justice on earth. Surely, then, worship planners will want to consider well the images used in worship.

Tapping the Imagination

Finding good images for worship means tapping the imagination. This can be done in various ways. Finding good images does not, however, mean creating from a void so much as it means fine-tuning our awareness. Poets bring fresh insights not by creating a different world but by carefully observing the world of daily experience. Rather than repeating inherited perceptions, they experience anew the stuff of daily life. Similarly, bringing imagination to the task of finding words for worship means being alert to God's presence in life experiences. Note how this dovetails with Christine Smith's concern that women bring their experiences to worship and the overall concern to speak contextually through the creative voice in worship. To be creative in worship, then, is not to seek novelty or cleverness for their own sakes but to incarnate faith with the textures and feelings of day-to-day Christian living. Imagination, then, involves a heightened awareness of life itself, attuned to God's mysterious movement within life.

Creative worship and preaching includes presenting content in visual or narrative form and not just through concepts. In a culture increasingly oriented to audiovisual rather than print media, thoughtful imagery not only retains people's interest but also offers an alternative to values often implied by cultural images.

Entering a scripture text freshly means closely noticing what is there, often through imaginative prayer that allows one to reenter the time and place that the passage portrays. Fortunately, many scripture texts are filled with imagery that can be highlighted in preparing prayers, hymns, and sermons. For example, the readings for the Third Sunday of Easter, year C, include many images. In Psalm 30, God raises someone "from the pit" and turns "mourning into dancing." The narrative in John 21 paints a picture with a boat, a big catch of fish, a charcoal fire by the sea, and a loaf of bread; the dialogue between Peter and Jesus speaks of expressing love for Jesus by "feeding his sheep." Acts 9:1–6 vividly tells the story of Paul's conversion; and Revelation 5:11–14 envisions hosts of creatures singing praise to Christ as the Lamb. Any of these texts present rich possibilities for images to develop in worship.

Brainstorming can also produce inspiring images for worship. Brian Wren helps people develop new images for God by group brainstorming based on the world of everyday life. The group takes an image such as shield, midwife, mother eagle, or wellspring, and calls out as many real life associations as possible. ("Don't think religiously!" Wren instructs.) What does a shield look like? What does it do? When is it used? Small groups develop a paragraph describing the image as fully as possible. Then group members write prayers focusing on one or more aspects of the description. This exercise helps writers to develop more vivid and engaging imagery.[15]

I recently wrote a new hymn for Pentecost. I brainstormed about several aspects of the Holy Spirit, and I finally chose an aspect not often explored in hymns—the mysterious power that renews and sustains life in the face of all challenges. I thought of ways this life force is expressed: the plant that grows through concrete or the voice of prophecy (like that of Nelson Mandela) that is not silenced by prison. I was reminded of the tenacity of characters in novels by Toni Morrison, Alice Walker, and Zora Neale Hurston and I thought of freedom marches for civil rights. These are images of the Spirit at work in daily life. I sought ways to speak about such experiences that would not be tied to events of 1994 and that would be intelligible to people who had not read the same books I had. Here is the hymn I wrote:

O Spirit, spring of hidden pow'r
that hallows day and night:
You are the force that prods the flow'r
through pavement toward the light.
You are the song that brings release;
in prison cell you do not cease.
Spring of pow'r, fire of love, giver of life:
come, renewing Spirit, come.

O Spirit of the holy cry
for human dignity.
You are the pride of head held high
before all bigotry.
Your rhythm rouses weary feet
to move to freedom's steady beat.
Spring of pow'r, fire of love, giver of life:
come, renewing Spirit, come.

O Spirit of undying life,
O breath within our breath:
You are the witness in our strife
that love surpasses death.
You are the gift that we desire;
anoint our heads with tongues of fire.
Spring of pow'r, fire of love, giver of life:
come, renewing Spirit, come.

Words: Ruth Duck, copyright 1994
Tune: JESOUS AHATONHIA
("'Twas in the Moon of Wintertime")

The imagery is open-ended enough to allow people to read a variety of experiences into the hymn. The hymn was sung for the first time at a Pentecost service at Garrett-Evangelical Seminary, as it happened, just after a heated debate about homosexuality erupted at the seminary. Some people appropriately read the cry of gay and lesbian people for human dignity into the second stanza of the hymn. Through the brainstorming process, I found fresh imagery that spoke to many in my worshiping community.

My process in writing the hymn for Pentecost demonstrates my approach to imagery for worship, regardless of how successful the hymn itself may be judged to be. By brainstorming, I came up with several possible directions for the hymn, then focused on a direction that had been least explored. Then I developed the hymn using imagery and experiences from daily life. I could have gone through a similar process had I started with a scripture text. In any case, brainstorming, focusing, and attending to everyday, concrete experiences inspires fresh imagery for worship.

Disciplined and creative imagery that draws on daily experiences of faith engages and inspires Christian communities. Imagery is central to the creative voice in worship. Although we are not all poets, all of us can listen, look, and feel more deeply, and thus we can assist the church to find words for worship better suited to the experience of faith.

5

Finding Words
to Preach

Preaching is central to worship, and many books have been written about the subject. These books can benefit any preacher, even one to whom preaching seems to come naturally, because multiple skills are needed for excellent preaching. In this chapter, I bring forward a small portion of this wisdom about preaching, not so much to present a new theory as to integrate some contemporary ideas about preaching with my overall concerns in this book. I also hope to assist seminarians or laity preparing to preach their first sermons. I also hope I help others by presenting preaching as a building block toward the goal of integrated and creative worship. I will explore choice of scripture, formation of a sermon, the creative process applied to preaching, and ways to integrate preaching and worship. First, though, I present a theology of preaching as a basis for the concrete suggestions that will follow.

A Theology of Preaching

Preaching is witness to God, who is present in all life, seeking us in love and calling us to lives of love and justice. Love often fails and injustice is powerful, both in the church and the world. Thus, preaching must name our human dilemmas honestly and bring both good news and challenge. Good preaching often names, and always has in mind, the human dilemmas that contemporary Christians experience in the global and local community. All persons and communities also need to hear good news, encouragement that nothing can separate us from the love of God, whose grace is sufficient for life's challenges (Romans 8:38–39). Good news includes hope, enabling us to imagine our lives more healed and whole, and the world more loving and just. To be complete, preaching must sound the challenge of the gospel, that persons transformed by hope and grace may live in love and justice toward God, neighbor, and ourselves. The good news empowers Christians to accept with hope and courage the challenge of faithful living. The challenge itself can be good news when it empowers people to work together with God's help to bring healing and justice on earth.

Scripture texts support all these dimensions of preaching. Scriptures present human dilemmas and failures with almost embarrassing honesty—from David's abuse of power in taking Bathsheba for himself, to the disciples' terror on a stormy sea, to church conflict. Scripture texts, speaking in terms of particular perspectives and cultures, witness to God's good news and challenge.

Other human experiences, past and present, are part of preaching's witness to the gospel. The "great cloud of witnesses" of the past testify with many voices to God's faithfulness and love (Hebrews 12:1). Contemporary experience also provides witness to God at work in particular contexts as Christians seek to be faithful.

Good preaching correlates the perspectives of scripture with the dilemmas and faith experiences of Christians past and present. Through preaching, Christians explore the resources that scripture and church tradition offer their lives. Mere exposition of scripture is not enough, for preaching must help people draw connections between the perspectives of scripture and their daily lives and relationship with God. Preaching therefore must go beyond even the exposition and application of insights from biblical passages. In good preaching, the world of the text and the world of today are put in dialogue with each other. In this way, scripture and contemporary experience illumine one another, helping us perceive who God is and what God is doing in the church, the world, and particular lives.

Preaching is a communal event. A sermon is not words on paper, but an event of communication in which both speaker and hearer participate. Contemporary preaching theory emphasizes awareness of how people listen to a sermon—how their thoughts progress, what keeps their attention, and what causes minds to wander or hearts to rebel. Whether listeners respond silently or through voices, faces, or body language, their response is as much a part of the preaching event as are the preacher's words. Thus, preaching is a two-part communication event involving both the meaning the preacher intends and the meaning hearers experience as they listen. Preacher and congregation create a sermon together.

Although a communal event, preaching also communicates truth through the personality of the preacher. Two examples will help here. In a church where I once served as interim pastor, a search committee was defining its hopes for a new pastor. Their last pastor had been so private about faith that her preaching was abstract and formal. The committee asked for a new pastor whose spirituality would be expressed in sermons that revealed the preacher's faith journey. But in another church, members complained that their pastor was always talking about himself in preaching. Both experiences reflect a conflict about the role of personal experience in current preaching theory. David Buttrick argues that preachers should disguise personal experience, if they use it, because calling attention to oneself can distract from the message.[1] Christine Smith, on the other hand, believes self-revelation builds relationship between preacher and congregation. Moreover, she argues, women who tell their story in preaching enhance a feminist theological perspective by claiming their "own lives as rich resources for religious understandings, wisdom, and insight."[2]

Preaching that does not grow out of personal conviction will not persuade others. Thus, I affirm Smith's view that stories from the preacher's life are integral to preaching. Experiences are shared for the sake of community to the glory of God. That means speaking of the full range of faith experience, rather than portraying oneself only as saint, sinner, or doubter. It means considering carefully whether a story from one's life best serves the purpose of a particular sermon or whether the search for illustrative material should continue. It means listening to and honoring the stories of all members of the congregation in their diversity, including children and youth, as well as of people in the global community. Preaching that honors diverse stories engages more hearers, helping them make connections with their lives.

The Holy Spirit also forges connections between preaching and human lives. The Holy Spirit moves in the preaching event as preacher and hearers prepare and as words are spoken and heard. As James Forbes, pastor of New York's Riverside Church, has said, the Holy Spirit works in preaching to call us to resurrection in a world where the power of death is strong.[3] Preaching can be part of the transforming work of the Spirit to bring justice and reconciliation in a troubled world. Through the Spirit, God speaks in preaching, whether through the best efforts of preachers or in spite of faulty preaching. This theological awareness brings humility: if preaching helps to transform lives, the transformation happens through the work of the Spirit in those who preach and hear.

Through Spirit-filled dialogue between the contemporary faith experience of preacher and hearers and dialogue with scriptures, preaching is part of God's transforming work through Jesus Christ in the Spirit.

Choosing Scripture
for Preaching

A lectionary, a list or book of scripture readings, is intended to lift out the texts most important to preaching and worship. The earliest lectionaries for Christian worship advised reading continually through a book in small portions each Sunday.[4] More recent lectionaries have tended to organize readings to address theological and liturgical concerns. For example, the Roman (Catholic) Lectionary of 1969 assigns Gospel readings as they fit the church year's celebration of the story of Jesus Christ and the church; other parts of the Gospels appear in the Sundays after Pentecost. In the Common Lectionary of 1983 and Revised Common Lectionary of 1992, some Protestant denominations adapted the Roman Lectionary to reflect their approaches to preaching, the church year, and scripture. Much preaching in Protestant churches presently follows the Revised Common Lectionary.

The Revised Common Lectionary provides for each Sunday readings from the Hebrew scriptures, Epistles, and Gospels, one or more of which will inspire the sermon. Psalms are also provided, not as preaching texts, but as resources for congregational worship. From the first Sunday of Advent until first Sunday after Pentecost, the readings complement each other, focusing on common themes.[5] For example, on the Second Sunday of Advent, year C, Malachi 3:1, "See, I am sending my messenger to prepare the way before me" (NRSV), coordinates with a reading from Luke 3:1–6 about John the Baptist, the messenger who prepared the way for Jesus. The lectionary provides two options for other Sundays after Pentecost. In one option, the three readings do not complement one another; instead, worship teams must choose to focus on one of three tracks: a sequence from a gospel, an epistle, or an extended narrative from the Hebrew scriptures (such as the story of Elijah). In the other option, the Gospel and Hebrew scripture coordinate.[6] Many churches have welcomed the Common Lectionary, because it provides such a broad range of scripture over a three-year period.

The value of lectionary use is debated. On the one hand, organizing preaching around a lectionary supports a more comprehensive use of scripture and nurtures the spirituality of the church year. To start with the lectionary is to be open to challenging scripture passages, rather than to choose texts that already support one's point of view. Using the lectionary may lead to better cooperation among worship leaders. For all these reasons, use of the lectionary can be very helpful.

On the other hand, some scholars argue that lectionary texts should, for a variety of reasons, be evaluated with care. For example, Justo González and Catherine Gunsalus González, in their book *Liberation Preaching*, ask preachers to note which texts and portions of texts the lectionary avoids.[7] Focusing on the lectionary readings encourages neglect of many scripture texts, including some justice-oriented texts, that are not included in the lectionary. They also ask preachers to question traditional interpretations and to approach texts by imagining the perspectives of the poor and powerless.[8] Christine Smith and Elisabeth Schüssler Fiorenza name the danger of allowing patriarchal perspectives in texts to stand unchallenged.[9]

One solution (if permitted in a denomination) is to consult the lectionary while planning services, but to claim freedom not to read

or preach from the texts. Another solution is to preach from difficult texts but also to consult the growing body of scholarship by
women and people of color that provide helpful new approaches to
evaluating and interpreting texts.[10] I believe that the lectionary can
be a helpful resource if used with care.

The churches that embraced the lectionaries of 1969, 1983,
and 1992 were generally those that felt the need to engage scripture
more deeply in preaching. Churches that keep scripture central in
preaching, yet do not follow the lectionary, select passages in a number of ways.[11] Some seek guidance from the Holy Spirit; others
search for passages that would address current concerns in the congregation or world. Still others follow the ancient practice of preaching through a book of scripture for several weeks or months, as a
way to deepen congregations' knowledge of scripture. Some
churches celebrate the church year without following the lectionary. In addition, a number of alternative lectionaries, some emphasizing peace and justice concerns, have appeared.

The degree to which one follows a lectionary in preaching and
organizing worship will differ according to the demands and theological orientations of denominations, local churches, and pastors.
But whatever the manner in which they select texts, each congregation and preacher should ask the following questions: Are we
reading a broad range of scripture passages over the years? Does
preaching address human needs, especially when the congregation
or nation is in crisis? Does the choice of texts bring forth the grace
and challenge of the gospel and support movement toward greater
love and justice in church and world? How can we be more open
to the Spirit as we choose and interpret texts for preaching? Whether
churches choose texts from the lectionary to emphasize in preaching, or choose all texts locally, they should consider how their patterns over time reflect their understanding of faith and mission.

The Sermon Form

Finding a fitting sermon form is crucial to good communication.
Good form keeps listeners' attention, by helping them follow the

sermon's progression. Faulty form can leave listeners wondering where the preacher is going or why particular material appears at all. Form determines whether sermons seem to flow smoothly, drag, lurch, or rush at breakneck speed.

Although few would deny that form is crucial for effective preaching, each historical period and religious community produces its own wisdom about the best preaching forms. Here I suggest several approaches because variety in form enhances preaching and because some forms are more effective depending on the content.

"Tell 'em what you're going to tell them. Tell 'em. Tell 'em what you told 'em." So goes a maxim that characterizes the preaching form Fred Craddock characterizes as "deductive."[12] In this method, a preacher states a proposition, then demonstrates it through a variety of strategies ("three points and a poem"), then restates it. This sermon form, favored by preachers in the first part of the twentieth century, is useful for sermons whose goal is primarily to teach; it helps hearers crystallize an idea. What this form sometimes lacks in interest, it gains through remembered content. When used along with other forms of preaching, the deductive sermon can contribute through sound teaching to a congregation's knowledge of scripture and Christian tradition.

In recent decades, however, teachers of preaching, including Craddock, have questioned the value of the deductive sermon on several grounds. For one thing, people tend to think and learn inductively; rather than beginning with a proposition that they prove or disprove, they explore several avenues, ponder and ruminate until insight emerges. Also, the deductive method assumes that clergy have information to dispense to laity who come to preaching with a blank slate, rather than seeing preacher and hearer as a team exploring truth together. While preachers surely do inform congregations through preaching, to preach is more than to transmit data. Further, various theological movements have influenced preaching. Theologies emphasizing metaphor inspire preaching centering on various images. Neo-orthodox theologians emphasizing God's mighty works, liberationists building theology out of histories of oppression, and others using experience as a primary theological source, all have contributed to the growing emphasis on narrative preaching.

Preaching may employ narrative in several ways. An extended narrative, often the story of a scripture character in the first or third person, may form the whole sermon. Like plays or movies set in other historical times, such sermons engage contemporary dilemmas through clues hidden in character, plot, or dialogue. Narrative sermons help scripture stories come alive, by helping the congregation identify with the people, personalities, or situations. At other times, narratives set in the present probe the dynamics of scripture passages by showing the same dynamics at work in a modern setting. When the whole sermon is a narrative, it does not state a point in so many words, but rather calls hearers to draw their own conclusions.

Even if a sermon is not an extended narrative, its overall form may resemble a narrative. Like a drama, a sermon may begin by setting the stage (of some life situation) and introducing particular human beings as protagonists. Then the dilemma emerges—some problem to solve, some need to address, some tension to embrace. The dilemma builds to a crisis, and then it is addressed through the presence and action of God. A brief denouement gives a closure of some kind—whether a full resolution of the crisis, or a final scene that allows the congregation to guess what will happen next. This way of creating sermons, for which Eugene Lowry is particularly noted, involves a progression that builds interest and leads dramatically and naturally to a conclusion.[13] The sermon that resembles an unfolding plot, like any other form, is more interesting when varied with other forms.

It is also possible thaat only part of a sermon will be in narrative form. Sermons may incorporate narratives from contemporary life, tradition, or scripture without the whole sermon being in narrative form. Instead of proving a proposition, such sermons may build to an insight gathered from exploration of concrete stories and examples. Narrative can provide the raw material of rumination, helping hearers to consider the realities of life and faith. As part of a larger sermon structure narratives may support both inductive and deductive sermons.

Sermons may also take poetic form. Preachers who enter imaginatively into the world of Isaiah may find themselves speaking rhythmically and developing images as done in the book of

Isaiah. Poetic sermons create a mood or intensify a perception. A poetic sermon that develops an image is probably at the opposite end of the continuum from the deductive sermon. The purpose of poetic sermons is not to convey new information but to bring fresh awareness of our lives and of God at work in them, through the senses of hearing, smell, taste, touch, or sight. A sermon developing the image of treasure in clay jars in 2 Corinthians 4:7–12 need not explain Paul's meaning, but rather evoke an experience of feeling fragile, yet bearing the precious gospel, through God's power at work in the church.

Varying sermon forms allows diverse people within a congregation to be engaged in the preaching event. Whatever the form, several principles hold. The beginning must engage attention and point toward the overall content of the sermon. The content must progress, moving people forward—whether by a plot unfolding or material organized in points that follow logically and clearly from one to the next. Cues at various points must signal movement, whether by storytelling devices or by transitional material that ends one movement and shifts to the next. The ending must bring together all that has been said in a brief and dramatic or pointed way that leads hearers toward daily life in God's presence. In all this, the preacher must imagine the hearers' response and ask: What will engage their attention? What will help them follow the sermon? What will help them leave worship more ready to live in faith? Form is essential to help hearers participate actively in the communication event of preaching.

The Creative Process and Preaching

Preaching grows out of the gifts and abilities of the preacher. Some preach better with a manuscript—others without.[14] Some excel at storytelling—whether from scripture, their own experience, or other human stories. Others develop their sermons through vivid imagery. Still others combine brief narratives and images into tightly woven structures. The task of preachers is not to model themselves after other preachers but to discover, develop, and discipline their unique abilities for preaching. Following the creative process in one's own way can help evoke each preacher's unique gifts.

The creative process also involves exegesis, helping the preacher understand the meaning and context of the text. I recommend beginning the process with prayer and engaging the imagination, and then doing exegesis before brainstorming. For me, by engaging the text before consulting scholars, I can let it speak freshly to me; then, by consulting scholars before beginning to focus the sermon direction, my approach can be grounded in knowledgeable interpretation of scripture. But people are different, of course, and starting with exegesis might be most effective for some people. In what follows, I apply the creative process described in chapter 2 to suggest a method for developing sermons.

Step One: Beginning with Prayer

Preparing sermons, like all our efforts to find words for worship, best begins in prayer. The Spirit can guide every stage of sermon preparation and delivery so that the message will address needs and challenges of which the preacher is not even aware. Through prayer, we renew our relationship with God and become more open to what God seeks to do through the preaching event. Regular prayerful preparation of sermons nurtures the preacher's spirituality; following the lectionary gives a Christ-centered rhythm to spiritual life.

Step Two: Engaging the Imagination

Engaging sense and experience helps the preacher connect scripture and contemporary life in an imaginative and lively way.

One way to enter into a scripture text is to pray the scriptures, imaginatively placing ourselves in the narrative, as I described in chapter 2. Many other possibilities exist. A text can be mimed— acted out through body movement. Role playing, in which each person in a group enters into the experience of a different character, can bring fresh insight. The dynamics of a text can be embodied in twentieth century garb. The movie *Jesus of Montreal* demonstrates this possibility. In it, an eager talent agent who promises the young protagonist all of Canada is Satan in modern dress. "Jesus" overturns the moneychangers' tables once more by upsetting the cameras and drinks of advertising executives who abuse female models. Such imaginative exercises help us enter into a text more fully, experiencing its human dynamics in a deeper, more contemporary way.[15]

Imagination also helps us portray contemporary experience vividly, rather than abstractly. The most effective preachers are alive to what is going on in the world around them; simple happenings at home, at work, or on a train become subjects for meditation on God's movements. Movies, novels, and even television commercials point toward dilemmas and questions that may preoccupy the hearers of a sermon. Engaging the senses by being aware of contemporary experience as well as scripture texts is part of preparing to preach.

Step Three: Brainstorming

Through brainstorming we consider several possible approaches to the main idea, form, and content of the sermon. The clustering method is invaluable in designing sermons. After doing exegesis and reflecting on related human experience, I may have many possible ideas floating in my head. Clustering helps identify how ideas relate to one another and which ideas are most important. A focus may emerge through intuition (the "aha" experience) or through conscious decision. Brainstorming helps preachers consciously consider several alternatives, rather than focusing prematurely on one.

Step Four: Focusing

Because of its length and oral nature, the sermon must be focused around one main idea, the message. Although the possibilities for a text may be rich and human needs may be diverse, a sermon can develop only one main idea effectively. This will almost always mean concentrating on only one scripture passage, even if three lectionary texts are read. A sermon idea is probably focused enough if we can state it in a short, noncompound sentence. If we have to use "and" or "but," we may have at least two sermons in mind.

Focusing also means tentatively choosing a form for the sermon.

Step Five: Let Words Flow

Whether one prepares in an oral or written way to preach, the rhythm of letting words flow, taking a break, then revising, is essential for effective preaching. Since preaching can be a vehicle for

God's work in human lives, the beginning preacher may be like Jeremiah, who was overwhelmed when called to speak for God, complaining that he did not know how to speak, for he was too young. Such respect for preaching, while appropriate, can block sermon preparation, so that no idea seems good enough. So, after choosing a focus, the next step in preparing a sermon is to silence the inner censor and let words flow—whether on paper or aloud.

Material need not be developed as it will be preached. For example, the main body of the sermon may be prepared before the introduction or conclusion, or the conclusion may be developed first. At times the sermon develops neatly according to plan; at other times, a new plan emerges during preparation. I once was preparing to preach about the story of Jesus' feeding of the multitudes in John 6:1–14. I intended to begin the sermon by speaking from the perspective of the boy who shared his loaves and fish, but the boy's story had a life of its own and became the whole sermon. I have learned that when a sermon takes a different direction than my plan, the Spirit may be at work.

Letting words flow at this stage of the process can help the preacher overcome blocks and remain open to what the Spirit is trying to say to a congregation through the sermon.

Step Six: Taking a Break

It can be tempting to leave sermon preparation until the last twenty-four hours before preaching, but beginning at least by the Monday before preaching on Sunday leaves time for what Richard Hoefler calls "incubation."[16] During the incubation period, sermon ideas are hatched. Many preachers find that if they do scripture study, brainstorming, and focusing several days before they preach, the sermon grows as they go about the week's activities. Preparing a draft a few days in advance also gives the distance needed for revision.

Step Seven: Revising

In early 1984, just before I left full-time parish ministry for graduate studies, I purchased a computer. In July, during farewell activities, our church president asked me, "Why are your sermons getting so much better, now that you're about to leave?" I answered that the computer allowed me to revise manuscripts to my heart's content. Earlier, I would give up before I felt finished, exasperated by the piles of crumpled paper at my feet. Now I was able to delete, add, or move things almost instantly, until the sermon was well crafted and easy to follow. Reflecting on this experience made me realize how important it is to revise sermons adequately, though, of course, a computer is only one tool for doing so!

Exciting preaching may seem deceptively like informal conversation. The expressive use of face, body, and voice and appropriate word choice make the preacher seem spontaneous and direct. Good structure and adequate oral practice make it seem that ideas are flowing effortlessly from point to point. To the listeners, a well-prepared sermon is like watching dancing by professionals. What looks effortless has taken years of learning and hours of hard work and practice. Taking the effort to prepare sermons helps listeners remain engaged and frees them from having to strain to follow the preacher's thought process. Then listeners can focus their effort on responding to the comfort and challenge of the gospel.

Evaluating a sermon-in-process may reveal the need to improve the overall structure of the sermon, choose words more carefully, or find more or better illustrative material. Looking at oneself in the mirror may lead to changes in gestures or body language. Listening to a sermon on tape can help us attend to the rhythm and sound of our speech. Noticing where the tongue wants to change wording will almost invariably improve the rhythm or naturalness of language. For this reason, revising a sermon must go hand-in-hand with oral practice, whether or not you will preach from a manuscript. Most of us must say things aloud to discover how they will sound. In all these ways, good preaching calls for careful, critical revision.

Step Eight: Learning from Feedback

Preaching does not end with sermon delivery. Since preaching is a communication event, you cannot improve as a preacher without learning what people heard and how it affected them. Congregations often give informal feedback, especially when a sermon "touched a nerve" by speaking to their deep concerns or by making them angry or upset. Preachers can learn a great deal by listening carefully to such feedback and asking questions to find out what was happening in their listeners.

More intentional feedback from a supportive but honest group that meets soon after a sermon is preached can be even more helpful. Areas to explore are: (1) what people actually heard; (2) whether good news came across; (3) what helped or hindered hearing; and (4) how this sermon will affect hearers' lives.[17] Such intentional feedback helps a preacher be more aware of the diverse human experiences that must be taken into account in order to deliver a message effectively.

While some are more naturally gifted in preaching than others, attending to neglected parts of the creative process can help anyone become a better preacher.

Integrating Preaching and Worship

Preaching focuses the creative voice in worship, giving a context and focus for the parts of a service that change weekly. Preaching approaches scripture texts and human dilemmas in a particular way, lifting out key concerns, images, and themes that can echo through worship, unifying a service. Even a short sermon (and sermons are, on the whole, shorter today than in the past) focuses worship around particular aspects of scripture and life. Thus preaching provides the thematic center for worship as it changes from week to week and season to season.

Sometimes Protestants have treated preaching as the main event of worship to which all else was preliminary; the rest of worship was, as it were, simply a frame to surround, or at best enhance the all-important picture. On rare occasions, something else would be the focus of worship, for example, an order for Holy Communion that left time only for a brief "communion meditation." A more wholistic approach is emerging today: preaching and other parts of worship *complement* each other, and both grow out of the texts and themes for the day. Thus other parts of worship echo and reinforce what has been said in the sermon, while preaching focuses the meaning of other parts of worship.

In these days of liturgical reform, preaching can support the experience of sacraments. The entire sermon need not focus on baptism or holy communion each time they are celebrated. Frequent preaching on the sacraments is, however, helpful in these times of reform. When Holy Communion follows preaching, the sermon appropriately points toward the table, given the multiple themes and images of communion. Some connections are obvious; the Gospels are full of stories of Jesus' sharing meals or feeding the multitudes. Other connections are more subtle: A sermon on accepting other humans in their diversity could speak of the communion table as the welcome table, echoing the African American spiritual, "I'm gonna sit at the welcome table."

Bringing out the baptismal dimension of texts, even on days when no one is baptized, encourages a congregation in their faith commitments. During the third and fourth centuries, faith communities would reflect during Lent on their baptisms, in solidarity with those preparing for baptism and first communion at the Easter vigil. The weeks of Pentecost (the Great Fifty Days, now called Eastertide) were a time for rejoicing in sacramental life. Lectionaries today recover these ancient practices by including ample references to the sacraments during Lent and Eastertide. Some are subtle, like the reference to new birth in John 3:1–7 or talk of being raised to a new life of love and unity in Ephesians 2:1–10. Bringing out baptismal references, even in passing, can nurture a congregation's sense of discipleship and Christian unity, and these references make baptism more meaningful when it is celebrated.

Preaching also can educate about other aspects of worship. There is always the danger of being didactic—for instance, by taking more time on the history of Epiphany than on its meaning for the faith and life of contemporary Christians. Attempts to educate should not overwhelm the theological purposes of preaching (naming, proclaiming good news, setting forth the challenge of living in faith). Changes in the worship environment, new hymns, and special celebrations can, however, be grist for the mill of sermon preparation. The preacher should always have in mind what else is happening in a worship service while preparing the sermon. A new banner can be the "hook" needed to engage hearers in an introduction. Special happenings in a service from renewal of wedding vows to recognition of church school teachers can provide sermon materials without diverting the message.

When preaching and worship are integrated, they reinforce one another. Preaching enhances the understanding and experience of other parts of worship; and other parts of worship echo and reinforce the sermon message.

Integration of preaching and worship calls for close cooperation between preachers and church musicians. Directors of music can best coordinate anthems with sermons if they know the scripture text and main idea or direction of the sermon, or at least the scripture. They should have this information at least six weeks in advance, since most choirs rehearse for several weeks before singing an anthem in worship. More time still is needed to purchase new music, should nothing in the anthem files be appropriate, so planning several months in advance is best.

Tensions exist, at times, between preachers and musicians. In their planning styles, many preachers do not show due respect and consideration to church musicians or for the coordination of preaching with the rest of worship. And some musicians have little interest in the overall content of worship. When musicians and preachers work together, however, a church is well on the way toward coordinated worship.

In addition to preachers and musicians, artists, church school teachers, and other congregation members should work together in planning worship and developing themes together. Like musicians, artists (such as those designing banners or choreographing movement) need time to design and develop visual art. Coordination with church school planners can involve children and youth more meaningfully.

Coordinated planning need not mean preparing full sermons weeks or months in advance, though some preachers do take a week in the summer to plan sermons for an entire church year. What I am suggesting is that preachers make basic plans for a group of six to ten services some weeks in advance. For example, in September, one would read all the lectionary texts for Advent and Christmas and develop a rough plan. The plan might identify what text would be central to each sermon and name a possible sermon direction, or even the main idea if it seemed clear. Ideally, this would be done in consultation with a worship committee, who also would consider other aspects of worship, such as hymns or visual art. The plan could be laid out in a one-page diagram and posted in a prominent place to guide all involved in designing the congregation's worship.

Preachers should coordinate their efforts with all others who have speaking parts in worship, so that they too can prepare whatever they will be doing. Far too often, field education students report that the senior pastor only assigns leadership roles while walking into the sanctuary immediately before worship. In desperation one student prepared everything but the sermon, if she knew the texts or themes for preaching. By year's end, she had learned to pray extemporaneously—a gift, for her, of field education. But pastors should show respect for both seminarians and laity by giving them at least a few days in advance the information they need to prepare. Even people who have a gift for extemporaneous prayer are more able to coordinate prayer with the rest of worship if they have the opportunity to mull over texts and themes.

The importance of the preaching ministry to worship is realized as preachers treat preaching and worship as a seamless whole and as they relate to other worship leaders as respected colleagues. The effort is worthwhile, even if it involves changing one's planning style, so that every part of worship has meaning in terms of the whole, echoing and elaborating the sermon message.

Creative preaching is essential to contemporary worship. It calls for great care as well as openness to the Spirit, who is active in all aspects of preparing, delivering, and responding to a sermon. Imaginative preaching complements prayer and singing as an expression of contemporary faith experience, witnessing to God who is present in all life and calling us to love and justice.

6

Forms of Prayer and Worship

Prayer is the encounter of the human creature with the Creator. As the language of relationship, prayer takes myriad forms; yet, several characteristic forms of prayer have emerged for corporate Christian worship. In this chapter, I explore briefly the history, theology, structure, and content of a few forms for prayer and worship. I discuss eucharistic prayers and hymns in chapters 7 and 8 because those topics require more detailed discussion.

Words to Begin Worship

Beginnings are important. The first sentence of a novel or the first scene of a movie engage (or fail to engage) our attention and create expectations for what is to come.

The beginning of worship is also important. Instrumental music, visual art, and the architectural space create expectations for worship before any words are spoken. An opening hymn involves a congregation in praising God. The first spoken words also help to set the tone and express the purpose of corporate worship: forming and renewing our relationship with God and one another through acts of praise, prayer, proclamation, and commitment.

Often the first words of worship are a *greeting* by a leader or between leader and congregation. Although in some churches, presider[1] and people begin by exchanging an informal "Good morning," other words can better indicate that the church meets in God's presence. For example:

P: God be with you.
R: *And also with you.*

Such a brief exchange may have been the entire opening ritual before reading scripture in early Christian worship.[2]

Greetings are often short scripture sentences, such as this one based on 2 Corinthians 13:13, which also serves well as a closing blessing:

P: The grace of the Lord Jesus Christ
    and the love of God
    and the communion of the Holy Spirit
    be with all of you.
R: *And also with you.*

Such greetings express Christian hospitality and acknowledge that the church gathers in God's presence.

At other times, the first words are an ascription of praise taken from scripture and spoken by the presider, such as these words of thanksgiving based on 1 Corinthians 15:12, 55, 57:

Christ has been raised from the dead.
"O death, where is your victory?
O grave, where is your sting?"
Thanks be to God,
who gives us the victory through our Lord Jesus Christ.[3]

Ascriptions of praise help congregations to begin worship by praising and thanking God. They may point us toward particular times or seasons of the church year; the one just quoted would be appropriate for a Sunday in Eastertide.

We also may begin by stating in whose name we worship, traditionally through a trinitarian formula such as "In the name of the Father and of the Son and of the Holy Spirit,"[4] or alternatively "In the name of God the Source, Word, and Spirit." The congregation responds, "Amen."

The *call to worship*, a closely related form of greeting, has emerged in the last few decades; it may come after the greeting or may include a greeting between worship leader and congregation. It includes a specific invitation to worship God together, for example, "Let us glorify the living God." In the call to worship, a worship leader may address the congregation, or the leader and congregation speak responsively. A call to worship may be based on scripture or contemporary experience. This call to worship for the third Sunday in Eastertide, year C, draws on several phrases from the psalm for the day (Psalm 30:4, 5b, 11, 12):

> LEADER: Sing praises to God, you faithful,
>   give thanks to God's holy name!
> PEOPLE: Weeping may linger for a night,
>   but joy comes in the morning.
> LEADER: You turn our weeping to dancing, God;
>   you remove the garments of mourning
>   and clothe us in gladness.
> ALL: May we praise you and not be silent!
>   We will give thanks to you, O God, forever![5]

Like the psalm, this call to worship begins as the leader addresses the congregation, then moves to praise of God by all. It uses scripture creatively by selecting key phrases and images, rather than by reciting a passage word for word responsively. A call to worship may refer to familiar narrative themes in the day's texts, if they can be understood before reading the texts. Poet and pastor Maren Tirabassi drew connections between the story of the magi found in Matthew 2:1–12 and contemporary experience in this call to worship for Epiphany:

> LEADER: The magi came from many places, following a star.
> PEOPLE: We come to worship, and the star sheds light on our lives.
> LEADER: The magi brought gifts to offer the Child.
> PEOPLE: We too bring gifts—ourselves, our hopes, our dreams.
> LEADER: Shepherds and magi—the meek and the mighty—all were welcome in Bethlehem.
> PEOPLE: We too come to Bethlehem and then return to our homes rejoicing.[6]

Here, the people state that they have come to worship, rather than the leader inviting them to worship.

A call to worship also may emphasize metaphors from everyday life. This poem by Mexican theologian Elsa Tamez serves as a good call to worship that one person would speak, for a service when Holy Communion will be celebrated:

Come on.
Let us celebrate the supper of the Lord.
Let us make a huge loaf of bread
and let us bring abundant wine
like at the wedding at Cana.

Let the women not forget the salt.
Let the men bring along the yeast.
Let many guests come. . . .

Come quickly.
Let us follow the recipe of the Lord.
All of us, let us knead the dough together
with our hands.
Let us see with joy
how the bread grows.

Because today
we celebrate
the meeting with the Lord.
Today we renew the commitment
to the Kingdom.
Nobody will stay hungry.[7]

The vivid imagery here comes from both scripture and everyday experience, metaphorically describing how Christians worship and work together in commitment to Jesus Christ and the reign of God.

Horace Allen, professor of worship, has parodied vacuous calls to worship that do not point to God but sound something like this: The leader asks, "Why are we here?," and the congregation responds, "We don't know." Allen's caricature points to the need to begin worship positively with vibrant affirmation of our faith. Unfortunately, most calls to worship that feature questions merely prompt the congregation to ask questions the worship leader wants to answer—a phony form of dialogue! Every word at the beginning of worship should have a certain dramatic evocative quality. A series of questions and answers seemed dramatic in the early 1970s, but seems less so now.

Still another form of prayer used at the beginning of worship is the *opening prayer*, also called the invocation.[8] Except on special occasions, the opening prayer should be brief. Through it, the congregation expresses praise and openness to God's transforming power in worship. According to a Disciples of Christ manual for worship,

"The opening prayer acknowledges the presence of God with the worshiping community and asks that those gathered may be receptive to the spirit, word, and action of God in the service."[9]

Opening prayers may invite God's presence or simply express the congregation's praise. The following opening prayer, which draws its imagery from Isaiah 35:1 and 6, expresses the community's longing for God:

> Creating and sustaining God,
> in your presence there is life.
> Living water springs up,
> and deserts blossom where you pass.
> Seeking the life that comes from you,
> we have gathered before you.
> Our hearts are ready, O God,
> our hearts are ready.
> Delight us with your presence,
> and prepare us for your service in the world;
> through the grace of Jesus Christ.
> Amen.[10]

Opening prayers may speak of gathering for worship and ask for God's presence (as this one does) or may simply express the community's praise. A worship leader may voice the opening prayer, or the congregation may pray in unison.

Christians begin worship in many other ways. These varied forms should not all be used in the same service, for worship should move rather quickly toward the scripture reading and sermon. An hour-long service that spends twenty minutes or more getting started is like friends who meet for lunch to discuss an important subject—which they avoid until their last few minutes together. Greeting one another and acknowledging that we are meeting in God's presence, the acts that begin worship, are simple, brief acts that set the context for all that follows.

The Collect:
A Classic Form for Prayer

A prayer form that is easy to learn and follow is the *collect*, which originated in early medieval times. Collect (pronounced col'-lect) literally means "assembly."[11] It traditionally came before the scripture readings and assembled or summarized prayers previously spoken; recent United Methodist and Presbyterian books of worship suggest using collects as opening prayers.[12] Preceded by a greeting between presider and people and concluded with a corporate "Amen," the collect was "a solemn summary by the president of the corporate prayer of the assembly."[13] In the sixteenth century it passed into Protestant tradition through Anglican Reformer Thomas Cranmer, who edited the first versions of *The Book of Common Prayer*. Cranmer translated Latin collects into English and composed new collects.[14] The collect, which may echo themes from the day or season of the church year is, however, defined by form more than content or placement. It can be used in varied times and seasons of worship; its simple, focused structure makes it a good form for people beginning to write their own prayers.

The collect form generally has five main parts. (1) It begins by naming God, and (2) tells what God does that makes that name appropriate. Then (3) the prayer makes a petition or request of God. Next (4) the prayer explains why the congregation requests this of God, or their hoped-for outcome; the clause usually begins with the word "that," leading into the purpose. The prayer closes with (5) words of praise. Collects are very brief, and at best, the parts fit together. The collect for Advent in the *United Methodist Hymnal*, adapted from *The Book of Common Prayer*, admirably shows the qualities of a collect:

1. Merciful God,
2. you sent your messengers the prophets to preach repentance and prepare the way for
    our salvation.
3. Give us grace to heed their warnings and forsake our
    sins,
4. that we may celebrate aright the commemoration of the
    nativity, and may await with joy
        the coming in glory of Jesus Christ our Redeemer;
5. who lives and reigns with you and the Holy Spirit,
    One God, for ever and ever. Amen.[15]

"Merciful God" names God in a way appropriate to the prayer's emphasis on repentance and salvation; the next clause remembers how God has already shown mercy to humanity, by sending messengers. The petitioners ask God to give them grace to heed the word of the messengers, "that" they may await Christ's coming with joy. Each part of the prayer is coordinated with the rest, except the final doxology, which conforms to the stylized ending of many collects in *The Book of Common Prayer.*

Collects historically have been only one sentence long, as shown here in a prayer by Janet Morley. In the collect above, the first sentence is a statement about God. Here, a subordinate clause describes God, and the main clause makes the request:

> God our healer,
> whose mercy is like a refining fire,
> touch us with your judgment,
> and confront us with your tenderness,
> that, being comforted by you,
> we may reach out to a troubled world,
> through Jesus Christ, Amen.[16]

This collect is admirable in its clear simplicity and in the way it brings together grace and judgment.

Those who compose new collects will want to avoid the picture of the human–God relationship that often seems to lie behind classic collects, the image of subject and ruler. Words such as "Almighty," "reigns," and "grant" echo royal court traditions; the form itself could be interpreted as a petition made quickly and deferentially, with reasons that it should be granted. Through vivid, thoughtful images of God and carefully coordinated phrases (and a doxology that is not stereotyped but fits the prayer), the collect can take on new life as a contemporary prayer form. When based on the scripture lessons, a collect can well follow the readings as a response to them.

Words Surrounding
Scripture Readings

The *prayer for illumination,* a brief prayer that precedes the reading and interpretation of scripture, is a gift to the whole church from the

Calvinist tradition. It follows Calvin's teaching that the Holy Spirit must illumine the congregation's understanding as scripture is read and interpreted, so that it will be the living word of God, motivating faithful discipleship in the world.[17] These intentions, rather than one classic form, shape the prayer for illumination, which typically includes, though not always in this order:

    a. address to God
    b. prayer that God will help us to hear and understand
    c. the word as read in scripture and proclaimed through preaching
    d. through the working of the Holy Spirit.

This prayer from the *United Methodist Hymnal* incorporates these classic elements of the prayer for illumination:

> Lord, open our hearts and minds
> by the power of your Holy Spirit,
> that, as the Scriptures are read
> and your Word proclaimed,
> we may hear with joy what you say to us today. Amen.[18]

The prayer for illumination also may ask that the word may bear fruit in our lives, as this prayer from *Thankful Praise* does with vivid imagery:

> O God, prepare the soil of our hearts
> so that as your Word is sown
> through reading and preaching
> it may take root, mature,
> and come to harvest in the life of the world.
> Through Jesus Christ, the sower of the seed. Amen.[19]

These two prayers are good models for composing prayers of illumination, which should, in any case, be brief.

The prayer before the scripture reading also may give thanks for scripture, as this one by Richard Allen, the founder of the African Methodist Episcopal Church, does:

> We believe, O Lord,
> that you have not abandoned us to the dim light of our own reason
> to conduct us to happiness,

but that you have revealed in Holy Scriptures whatever is necessary
for us to believe and practice.
How noble and excellent are the precepts,
how sublime and enlightening the truth,
how persuasive and strong the motives,
how powerful the assistance of your holy religion.
Our delight shall be in your statutes,
and we shall not forget your Word. Amen.[20]

Allen's prayer is eloquent, not so much through imagery as through its piling up of adjectives and parallel phrases in the second sentence and through its spirit of devotion and trust.

In its varied forms, prayer before scripture, and not just before the sermon, emphasizes the participation of the whole people of God in hearing and interpreting the word.

The words immediately before and after scripture readings also matter. The words before the reading should name the book and chapter, and usually the verses; a sentence or two should set the context of the passage, to help hearers focus their thoughts.[21] It is good also to replace pronouns at the start of passages with names. Thus, the introduction to Matthew 4:18–22 could begin: "The scripture reading this morning is from Matthew 4:18–22" or "Listen for the word of God in Matthew 4:18–22" or "Listen to the Gospel of Jesus Christ according to Matthew 4:18–22".[22] Next, the context would be described: "Here, after Jesus has been baptized and tempted, he begins his ministry by calling the first disciples." The actual reading would begin: "As *Jesus* [not "he," as in NRSV] walked by the Sea of Galilee. . . ." Words after the reading can be as simple as, "Here ends the reading. Thanks be to God." They could draw on the passage: "This is the gospel. May we, too, rise up and follow when Christ calls." Or, the reader may follow a Gospel reading with such words as "This is the good news of Jesus Christ." The congregation could respond, "Thanks be to God."

The Act of Confession

Writing prayers of confession (and doing it well) is challenging. I begin, then, by alerting would-be writers of the challenges of writing prayers of confession.

Few if any Christians would claim to be free from sin, but we experience sin in many ways. A unison prayer of confession must name our sin in a way general enough to be honest for entire worshiping congregations. Unison confession of sin, which became possible after the invention of the printing press, grew out of the Reformation concern about abuses of priestly power in private confession. After Vatican II, the Roman Catholic Church experimented with corporate confession, but Roman authorities soon decided that it should not replace individual naming of sin to a priest. Meanwhile, some Christians have sought other means of "conversion therapy" (the process of turning away from sin toward lives fully committed to love of God and neighbor) that involve personal storytelling and support for changing one's life. Spiritual direction or twelve-step groups are examples.

Various liberation theologies have challenged the church's understanding of sin and grace in a way that, if taken seriously, would change the way we talk about sin and grace in worship. Several feminist theologians have argued that people may experience sin differently because of different gender role expectations or because of differences in social or political power.[23] For example, some women and men may hurt themselves and others more through lack of self-affirmation and self-care than through excessive pride and selfishness, sins often confessed in worship.

Andrew Sung Park, a Korean American liberation theologian, challenges the way Western theology and worship emphasize reconciliation between God and sinner, without calling for justice and healing for the victims of sin. Christian liturgies do little to resolve what Koreans call *han*, deep-seated feelings of powerlessness, repressed anger, and self-hatred growing out of oppression. Worship that dealt effectively with the power of sin in human life would promote the healing of victims, the conversion of oppressors, and the justice without which true reconciliation cannot happen.[24] Park's observations raise questions about the frequency and content of the act of confession. His exploration of *han* suggests a large area of human experience that Christian liturgy often ignores.

Liberation theologies ask the church to address the sin not only of individuals but also of societies. Yet how does one write a unison prayer of confession, when oppressor and oppressed intertwine not only in one congregation, but often in one person, who may both suffer injustice and do injustice to others?

Given these challenges, local churches may want to seek new ways of conversion therapy or use classic prayers of confession. Almost everyone can say honestly with *The Book of Common Prayer* that we have sinned against God "in thought, word, and deed, by what we have done, and by what we have left undone."[25] The words of a psalm (such as Psalm 51) or hymn may also lend themselves well to common confession. But here are guidelines for the act of confession for local churches that are bold enough to write their own prayers.

Prayers of confession are part of a larger structure that moves from a call to confession to a time of silence for individual reflection and a unison prayer (the unison prayer may precede the silence). An expression of God's forgiveness (variously called absolution, declaration of forgiveness, words of grace, assurance of forgiveness, among other names) follows, then a response of praise and thanksgiving. The whole sequence helps congregations prepare for confession, confess, accept God's forgiveness, and respond in thanksgiving. Given Park's critique, a charge to turn to lives of love, justice, and reconciliation might follow the expression of forgiveness. Especially when the act of confession follows the sermon and precedes Holy Communion, it may end with the passing of peace as an act of reconciliation before bringing the gifts of bread and cup to the table. Not every act of confession need include the entire sequence, but parts should fit together, and leaders should give confident witness to God's grace whenever congregations confess.

The United Methodist Book of Worship suggests this sequence for the act of confession in a service of word and table:

INVITATION

Christ our Lord invites to his table all who love him,
who earnestly repent of their sin
and seek to live in peace with one another.
Therefore, let us confess our sin before God and one another.

PRAYER OF CONFESSION

[The text of the prayer is provided below]

All pray in silence.
PROCLAMATION OF FORGIVENESS
Leader to people:
   Hear the good news:
      Christ died for us while we were yet sinners;
      that proves God's love for us.
   In the name of Jesus Christ, you are forgiven!
People to leader:
   In the name of Jesus Christ, you are forgiven!
Leader and people:
   Glory to God. Amen.
THE PEACE
   Let us offer one another signs of reconciliation and love.[26]

This order models mutuality between clergy and laity, who speak words of forgiveness to one another. Those who have theological objections to clergy absolving laity should follow this mutual model, rather than to withhold words of forgiveness and grace that are essential in an act of confession. Note that there are many alternatives to the brief response, "Glory to God. Amen"; many churches follow the witness to God's forgiveness with the Doxology or other song of praise.

The prayer of confession itself has a classic structure:

1. Address of God, which may stress God's grace or refer to a scripture passage previously read in the service.
2. An acknowledgment of our sin and brokenness ("we confess," "we admit," "we acknowledge" . . .)
3. A specific naming of sin, which may be general, like the prayer of confession from *The Book of Common Prayer* quoted above, or specific to the day's scriptures or concerns.
4. A request for forgiveness and transformation.
5. A statement of hope . . .
6. Through God named in the prayer.

The prayer of confession from the United Methodist sequence just cited follows the pattern:

(1) Merciful God,
(2)   we confess (3) that we have not loved you with our
         whole heart.
       We have failed to be an obedient church.
       We have not done your will,
         we have broken your law,
         we have rebelled against your love,
         we have not loved our neighbors,
         and we have not heard the cry of the needy.
(4) Forgive us, we pray.
(5) Free us for joyful obedience,
(6) through Jesus Christ our Lord. Amen.[27]

This prayer demonstrates a simple structure for prayers of confession that name our sin and our hope in God's transforming grace. Other structures are possible. Leader and congregation may speak prayers of confession responsively; or the congregation may have a repeated response to phrases of confession spoken by the leader. For example, a litany of confession based on the Ten Commandments might begin:

> LEADER: Holy God, you command us to hold no other gods before
>   you, yet we worship the things our hands have made.
> PEOPLE: God, forgive us, and write your law on our hearts.

The congregation would respond with the same words each time as the leader spoke words of confession related to each commandment.

The act of confession may take place at the beginning of a service, or it may follow scripture reading and sermon. Prayers of confession placed early in a service should be quite general. Prayers of confession that are locally created should generally follow the scripture readings and sermon and coordinate with the concerns they express. The Presbyterian *Book of Common Worship* provides an excellent example of a prayer of confession based on a particular passage of scripture (Acts 2:1–13):

> Almighty God,
> you poured your Spirit upon gathered disciples
> creating bold tongues, open ears,
> and a new community of faith.

We confess that we hold back the force of your Spirit among us.
We do not listen for your word of grace,
speak the good news of your love,
or live as a people made one in Christ.

Have mercy on us, O God.
Transform our timid lives by the power of your Spirit,
and fill us with a flaming desire to be your faithful people,
doing your will for the sake of Jesus Christ our Lord.[28]

This would be a good response to a sermon about the coming of the Spirit to the church. A sermon on a topic such as homelessness or violence might be followed by a litany of confession exploring the way we take part in or contribute to these realities.

The more specific the confession, the more room is needed for different experiences. For example, in relation to violence, some congregation members could honestly confess physically violent acts, others could confess failure to confront violence, and still others could confess benefiting from social injustice that breeds violence. We can honor the variety of experiences in several ways. Words like "if" or "when" are useful:

"If we have abused any human being, God, forgive."
"When we fail to confront violence around us, God, forgive."

Or, a time of silence for self-examination might be better than printed words to enable prayer about such a charged issue. Phrases such as "sometimes we . . .; at other times we . . ." or "some of us . . . ; others of us . . ." also can make room for the varying experiences highlighted by liberation theologians:

Gracious God,
we confess that we do not know ourselves as you know us.
Sometimes we esteem ourselves too highly,
heedless of the hurt we cause to you and to others.
Sometimes we esteem ourselves too little,
failing to rejoice in the gifts
you bestow on us.
Forgive our illusions of grandeur or self-hatred;
through your grace, free us to be the persons you intend,
through your Spirit at work among us. Amen.[29]

Locally created prayers of confession are often less balanced than more general prayers, repeating hackneyed phrases, such as those that emphasize only excessive pride. Writing prayers of confession for a given time or place calls for freshness of expression with loving sensitivity to the actual persons who will pray the prayer. When writing unison prayers of confession, picture the persons who will pray the prayer. Can they honestly speak it? Those who write prayers of confession also should take special care not to fall into the preaching mode. Preaching or small group dialogue can address controversial issues, but people who do not agree that something (such as our nation's latest military intervention) is wrong should not be forced to say so in prayer. Obviously, this requires understanding the congregation; one church may readily judge the war to be wrong and admit complicity in it, but another may not. Even in a congregation that generally agrees on issues, dissenters usually exist. They may accept the majority view more through dialogue than through the coerced agreement that locally created prayers of confession sometimes promote.

Finally, unison prayers of confession should usually be quite brief. An analogy may help. When we tell a loved one that we were wrong, the simple words "I'm sorry I did it" often express deep feelings and lead to reconciliation more than long speeches. Similarly, prayers of confession can often express the honest feelings of a congregation more powerfully when focused and concise. Excess verbiage and rambling prose may blunt rather than heighten genuine repentance and hope for transformation.

Prayers of confession are, I believe, the most difficult form of prayer to compose with adequate sensitivity and grace. At the same time, locally created prayers of confession can be meaningful, particularly when they grow out of the themes of scripture and sermon. Given the depth of human sin, suffering, and injustice in our time, the ministry of conversion therapy is essential. I hope this brief discussion will encourage those who compose prayers of confession to do so with great care.

Prayers of the People

The prayers of the people (also known as the intercessions or the prayer of the faithful, among other names) take many forms, but ever since the earliest churches, Christians at worship have prayed for the church and the world. This form of prayer brings human need before God in hope, trust, and thanksgiving for God's faithfulness. It includes prayer for the church, for all humanity, and for all creation, as well as prayers for one another in the local community of faith. Here, liturgy and life come together; thus, in church tradition, a deacon or layperson involved in ministry in the world has often led all or part of the prayer. Even churches that use denominational prayers elsewhere in the service often prepare intercessions locally week by week in order to offer particular needs, griefs, and concerns to God. In silent, locally prepared, or spontaneous prayer, congregations name their concerns, whether for an end to violence in Bosnia or for healing for a church member after surgery. Christians pray with confidence that God cares about our real human lives with their suffering and joy and that God is at work in the world to bring about healing, love, peace, and justice.

The author of 1 Timothy asks that "supplications, prayers, intercessions, and thanksgivings be made for everyone, for rulers and all who are in high position, so that we may lead a quiet and peaceable life in all godliness and dignity" (1 Tim. 2:1–2, NRSV, adapted.) Like other early Christian writers, Justin Martyr, teacher of the church in second-century Rome, mentions common prayer: "We offer prayers in common for ourselves, for [the one] who has just been enlightened [baptized], and for all [people] everywhere."[30] Clement, bishop of Rome, provides us with the following intercessory prayer, written in the late first century:

Save the afflicted among us,
have mercy on the lowly.

Raise up the fallen,
show yourself to those in need.

Heal the sick,
and bring back those who have strayed.

Fill the hungry,
give freedom to our prisoners,

Raise up the weak,
console the fainthearted.[31]

In the first five centuries of the church, the intercessions usually came after the sermon and before Holy Communion. By the fourth century, the intercessions became part of the eucharistic prayer in some regions, because "the idea developed that such intentions and intercessions were more effective if they were imbedded in the eucharistic prayer."[32] The fifth-century Roman mass borrowed from the Eastern church to include the kyrie eleison ("Lord, have mercy") after each petition. In later Roman liturgies, only the kyrie remained, without intercessions, until they were restored after Vatican II. During the Reformation, most Protestant churches recovered intercessory prayers, in printed litanies (Lutheran and Anglican) or in extemporaneous pastoral or congregational prayer (Puritans, Baptists, and others). Most churches today include some form of the prayers of the people in their worship.

The prayers of the people (in varied forms) usually begin with an invitation to prayer. Then prayers of intercession typically express concern for the church, the world, and their leaders; for the poor, the troubled, the sick, and the grieving; and for peace and justice. They also may include prayers for the departed, for families, for children, and for the harvest. Some center around particular themes. Richard Mazziota has prepared a set of intercessory prayers based on texts from the three-year lectionary;[33] for example, his intercessions for Christmas Eve include a prayer for unwed mothers.

Technically, prayers for others are intercessions and prayers for ourselves are petitions; either can be called a prayer "intention." Intercessory prayers do, in fact, include petitions for congregations and individuals within them.

Some congregations participate freely in extemporaneous intercessory prayers, in no particular order, after an invitation by a worship leader. Each petition or intercession may end with the same phrase that leads to a common response. For example, the individual prayer may end with "God, in your wisdom" or "Lord, in your mercy," and the congregation may respond, "Hear our prayer." (The prayer leader should be prepared to say the words leading to the common response such as "God, in your wisdom" when community members neglect to end their prayers with the cue phrase.) A worship leader may close with a prayer (perhaps in collect form) that brings all the individual prayers together.

The *bidding prayer* is another very common (and ancient) form of the prayers of the people. The word "bidding" means "prayer" in Anglo-Saxon.[34] In a bidding prayer, a worship leader asks the people to pray about a particular concern in silence. Another worship leader concludes the time of silence with a brief prayer about that concern. Then the process is repeated with the remaining intentions. Traditionally, a deacon or another layperson has voiced the biddings, while the presiding minister has prayed following each time of silence; in any case, it may be good to involve more than one speaker. The prayer may close with an expression of thanksgiving and trust in God.

Each bidding may be followed not only by silence but with brief extemporaneous prayers. For example, the leader could say, "Let us pray for peace in those places where war or violence threaten or destroy human lives." The congregation could name specific countries presently at war, particular human contexts (such as homes where children or elders are being abused), or nearby areas where violence has been happening recently. Or the leader could say, "Let us pray for those in need of healing," and the congregation could name persons who are ill.

Intercessory prayers may be in litany form; that is, a worship leader may pray for each intention and close with a common phrase, to which the congregation responds. For example, the presider's part in Mazziota's prayer for the Feast of the Epiphany ends with "We pray to the Lord"; the people respond, "Lead us to glory."[35] One problem with this approach is that the people always have the repeated (perhaps boring) part. Walter C. Huffman addresses this problem by suggesting that congregations who do intercessory prayer in litany form use a repeated response within each prayer, but that the response be varied from Sunday to Sunday.[36] Another approach is to sing either the whole prayer or the responses. *Praise God in Song,* a book of orders for daily prayer, offers an interesting alternative: a cantor chants each intention, and the people sing the response, "Lord, have mercy," humming the final chord quietly, while the cantor continues.[37]

The bidding prayer provides a good opportunity to honor varied languages in a congregation. Mark Francis suggests that the presider alternate languages after each time of silence; the concluding prayer could be in the language of the majority.[38] When bidding prayers include brief extemporaneous prayers by the community, it would be good to invite people to pray in their first language. A common response at the end (e.g., "God in your wisdom") could use one of the languages spoken in the community on one Sunday, another language on a different Sunday. Or the person praying could say, "Kyrie eleison" ("Lord, have mercy"), and the congregation could respond, "Christe eleison" ("Christ, have mercy"), thus using Greek, a language of ancient Christian worship, but perhaps not of any group within the community.

Intercessory prayers may be responsive; that is, leader and congregation may alternate in expressing intentions. The whole assembly must have a copy of the prayer in a worship book or bulletin, but less time is spent in repeated phrases. The responsive form is especially useful when a special occasion calls for numerous intentions; it may save time and engage the congregation more actively.

Jeremiah Wright, pastor of a dynamic African American church in Chicago, has said that in vibrant, growing churches, people share their stories, pray for one another, and testify to God's grace in their lives.[39] His comments suggest that whatever form intercessory prayers take, they should incorporate the present joys and concerns of the worshiping community, so that they may rejoice with one another's joys and weep with one another's sorrows (Romans 12:15). Extemporaneous intercessory prayer serves this purpose well, as do bidding prayers with brief intentions. Deacons, prayer groups, or members of lay ministry programs can compose litanies and responsive prayers based on needs they discover in a congregation. Intercession is a ministry of the whole church, calling for the prayer of the whole people of God, with trust in and thanksgiving to the God who lives and moves within human lives.

The Pastoral Prayer

The pastoral prayer is a familiar part of twentieth-century Protestant worship. In second-century Rome, the whole congregation lifted up its prayers and intercessions, according to Justin Martyr.[40] The Great Prayer of Thanksgiving, also called the eucharistic prayer, was the one prayer assigned to the ordained (bishops or priests) at that time, and for much of church history. The roots of the pastoral prayer, as practiced in many U.S. Protestant churches, are in the Puritan and frontier traditions, with their emphasis on free, spontaneous, and locally prepared prayer, as opposed to set liturgies.[41] In the seventeenth, eighteenth, and early nineteenth centuries, laity often participated in free prayer, if only to write notes to the pastor with prayer requests.[42] Prayer in the frontier tradition featured less lay participation and greater emphasis on the conversion of sinners. Pastoral prayers in the early twentieth century were not so often revivalist in content, but, at their best, an art form as eloquent and well-prepared as any sermon. Luminaries such as George Buttrick and Peter Marshall attracted large congregations not only because of their excellent preaching but also because of their well-crafted, deeply pious, pastoral prayers.[43] Riverside Church pastor Harry Emerson Fosdick wrote that "leading a congregation in public prayer is a work of art, demanding expert skill and painstaking preparation,"[44] and his published prayers demonstrate such care. By the late 1960s, however, pastoral prayers were known more for the congregation's labor in listening than pastors' care in preparation. Judging from worship manuals of the 1960s, too many pastoral prayers wandered aimlessly, reflecting the pastor's individuality more than corporate prayer, with an exasperating repetition from Sunday to Sunday.[45] One frustrated youth group timed the pastoral prayer one Sunday at twenty-seven minutes![46]

Not surprisingly, given this checkered past, books of worship today tend to minimize the pastoral prayer. *The Book of Common Worship* (of the Presbyterian Church, U.S.A., and the Cumberland Presbyterian Church) appears never to mention pastoral prayers. Other books and manuals of worship assume that the pastoral prayer will be intercessory in content. One such volume, the *United Methodist Book of Worship*, gently advises leaders to seek alternatives to the pastoral prayer: "Corporate prayer . . . should avoid lengthy discourses. Silent prayers, bidding prayers, and prayers of petition are excellent alternatives to a traditional pastoral prayer."[47]

Those who prepare denominational worship books and manuals are still wary of careless, lengthy, general pastoral prayers that are not corporate in nature. For example, Disciples of Christ leaders writing in *Thankful Praise* advise:

> When the prayer is offered by one person, he or she must prepare carefully so that these words become truly a prayer of the people and not a mini-sermon directed from the leader to the people. . . . Specific, concrete, evocative language and imagery . . . will lead the . . . congregation to pray out of the specific and concrete realities of their own lives.[48]

Traditionally a pastoral prayer might include adoration, confession, thanksgiving, intercession, petition, and commitment. Today these topics are more often subjects for different prayers, some of which include active congregational participation, while pastoral prayers generally focus on intercession.

In free churches today, the pastoral prayer is often based on intercessions gathered from the congregation. Congregations sometimes present their thanksgivings and concerns to the worship leader in writing either in a notebook that ushers bring forward before the pastoral prayer or on index cards that ushers organize into categories. Joys and concerns also can be spoken by the congregation spontaneously as part of worship, for a leader to weave into prayer. This is most effective when the congregation is small enough and the acoustics good enough for members to hear one another. Otherwise, the leader often attempts to repeat the prayer requests verbatim, first as an announcement, then in prayer. The result is often either wordy repetition that impedes the flow of the service or awkwardly bungled names and concerns. Further, the time of naming prayer requests easily becomes a general announcement period—I once heard someone advertise an apartment for rent during the joys and concerns! In contrast, the approaches to intercession in the previous section have much to commend them. The people voice their prayers (in silence or speech), engaging in the priesthood of all believers. Energy is focused on prayer rather than on gathering information. Further, the church's intercession should encompass a broad range of concerns for the church and the world; spontaneous joys and concerns very often focus almost entirely on individual local needs. When the pastoral prayer centers on spontaneously named joys and concerns, leaders must exercise care in keeping the whole event as simple and prayerful as possible, with concern for healing, justice, and peace both within and beyond the congregation.

Another contemporary model for pastoral prayer is the "prayer for the day"—brief, focused prayer growing out of the scriptures, themes, and images of a particular worship service.[49] Such a prayer might well be no longer than two minutes, following thirty to sixty seconds of silent prayer. This prayer could follow the sermon, though it should differ from the sermon not only in being addressed to God but also in its intention to express the prayer of the whole congregation. Such pastoral prayers require careful preparation, perhaps in writing, always with a prayerful focus on the needs of the congregation and the world, as well as with consciousness of the direction of the rest of the service.

Some pastors combine the prayer for the day with intercessory prayer based on spontaneously expressed joys and concerns. To the congregation's joys and concerns, the pastor adds thanksgivings and intercessions related to the themes and images of the day. Thus, each pastoral prayer is specific both to what is shared spontaneously and to what is happening in a particular worship service.

The pastoral prayer is in a state of change at this time, yet I can risk offering a few guidelines. Like all prayers, the pastoral prayer should address God, speak from authentic faith experience, and avoid trite or stereotyped phrases. Its language should, as George Buttrick wrote in 1942, be "movingly human and plainly reverent."[50] Classic liturgical prayers and outstanding pastoral prayers can provide inspiration for tone and language.[51]

The pastoral prayer should be well organized so that a congregation can follow easily. Those who lead a congregation in prayer should prepare carefully, perhaps in writing, certainly in reflection and prayer. George Buttrick argued that a pastor who had to choose between preparing the prayer and the sermon "might better forget the sermon," since the greatest need people bring to worship is to open their lives to God.[52] Yet the goal should not be eloquent performance (lest congregations think that only those with a seminary education can pray), but expression of a living relationship with God.

Above all, the pastoral prayer should be understood as a corporate act. A worship service should include not only a pastoral prayer but also times when the congregation can speak its own prayers. Thus, the pastoral prayer should be brief in order to allow time for the congregation's spoken prayers. The pastoral prayer itself is not the private devotion of the leader. It is an attempt to voice in a specific way the deep longings of the congregation for themselves, those they love, and the world so that the prayer becomes *their* prayer. This means that leaders should allow ample time for silence, at the beginning (so that everyone can enter the spirit of prayer), during intercessions (so that people can pray for unspoken needs), and in short pauses at appropriate points that allow the congregation to stay in tune with prayer. Because the pastoral prayer is corporate, it should not include the act of confession; people must be given the choice whether to pray the prayer, and God's grace should always be proclaimed in immediate connection with confession. Developing the practice of having the congregation say, "Amen" or placing the Prayer of Jesus (traditionally called the Lord's Prayer) at the end is another way to express the corporate nature of the pastoral prayer.

The pastoral prayer is a hardy plant that resists attempts by experts to weed it out and replace it with other forms of prayer. Prayer by ordained leadership indeed has a rightful place in corporate worship. Through visits in homes, hospitals, and coffee shops, pastors come to know the needs of a whole congregation. In these and other ways, the ordained symbolically represent and express the whole church's caring for individuals and the world. Pastors who practice a vital relationship with God in prayer can help their congregations learn to pray, through the authenticity of their public prayers. If prepared with care and corporate consciousness, the pastoral prayer can be the prayer of the whole worshiping community.

Words to End Worship

The words that end worship serve two theological purposes. First, they charge the people to live faithfully as Christians in the world. Horace Allen writes: "All that has happened in the assembly by way of praise, confession, proclamation, prayer, and thanksgiving is now, in the final moments of worship, directed toward daily praise and dedicated obedience in the common life."[53] Second, the closing words of worship send people out with a blessing in God's name, reaffirming the witness to the gospel that has already taken place in the service. A closing hymn or prayer may serve these purposes, but usually worship leaders also speak words of charge and blessing.

A charge (or "commissioning") encourages people to live as Christians in the world. A blessing (or "benediction," a word that means "blessing," drawing on Latin roots) assures people of God's love, grace, and saving power. Often, a deacon has given the charge, as an extension of the ministry of service in the world. It often makes sense for the preacher to give the blessing, as an extension of the ministry of proclaiming the gospel. Tradition has often reserved the blessing for clergy; yet laity, like clergy, can proclaim God's grace and blessing, if not forbidden by denominational policy or law. The point is to send worshipers into the world both with a challenge to live faithfully and with assurance that God's grace will empower them to do so. The charge may follow or precede the blessing.

The following charge, based on several passages of scripture, seems also to echo the prayer of Clement of Rome quoted above:

> Go out into the world in peace;
> have courage;
> hold on to what is good;
> return no one evil for evil;
> strengthen the fainthearted;
> support the weak, and help the suffering;
> honor all people;
> love and serve the Lord,
> rejoicing in the power of the Holy Spirit.[54]

A charge also could echo one of the scripture readings for the day or the sermon. For example, this charge, which echoes 1 Peter 2:9, would be appropriate when that passage is read:

> You are a chosen people,
> a royal priesthood,
> a holy nation,
> God's own people.
> Go into the world in peace,
> declaring the praises of God
> who has called you.[55]

The charge, in one way or another, challenges us to live as Christians in the world.

The blessing or benediction sends people out assured that God loves and empowers them with grace. Many blessings come from scripture; for example, the Presbyterian *Book of Common Worship* offers blessings that quote or adapt Hebrews 13:20, 21; Philippians 4:7; 1 Thessalonians 5:23;[56] 2 Corinthians 13:13; and Numbers 6:24–26, as well as this blessing from Romans 15:13:

> May the God of hope
> fill you with all joy and peace in believing,
> so that you may abound in hope
> by the power of the Holy Spirit. Alleluia! Amen.[57]

Blessings may be trinitarian:

> You are God's servants gifted with dreams and vision.
> Upon you rests the grace of God like flames of fire.
> Love and serve the Lord in the strength of the Spirit.
> May the deep peace of Christ be with you,
> the strong arms of God sustain you,
> and the power of the Holy Spirit strengthen you
> in every way. Amen.[58]

These two blessings call for the people to respond, "Amen."

At times, the charge and blessing are combined, perhaps in a responsive form. This "Commissioning and Benediction" emphasizes charge but ends on a note of blessing. It gracefully challenges people to be faithful through life's changes:

> LEADER: Let us go forth into the new seasons of our lives.
> PEOPLE: We go forth into growing and changing and living.
> LEADER: Let us go with caring awareness for the world and all that is in it.
> PEOPLE: We go to discover the needs and opportunities around us.
> LEADER: Let us go forth in peace and be led out in joy.
> ALL: We go in God's continuing presence, with the power to love and the strength to serve. Amen.[59]

The closing words of worship also may be in the form of a litany in which a worship leader sends the congregation out by speaking short phrases to which the people respond, "Thanks be to God." Worship leaders should speak the blessing confidently, preferably from the front of the church with good eye-contact, to encourage the congregation's faith as they return to their daily lives.

Christian prayer takes myriad forms, far beyond those described in this book. Time-tested forms need not restrict the expression of heartfelt prayer. Instead, when used honestly and imaginatively, they can help express a congregation's praise and longings. Tradition has provided the forms; we can concentrate on the content of what we need to say to God and one another in this time and place.

7

Thanksgiving at the Table: Prayers for Holy Communion

Jesus followed the Jewish tradition of thanking God for food, drink, and the gifts of life as he led the shared meals so central to his ministry. Our eucharistic prayers—prayers of thanksgiving at the table of Christ before distribution of the communion elements—grow out of this simple act of giving thanks. The word "eucharistic" comes from the Greek word *eucharistia,* which means "to give thanks." The prayer at table is called "the Great Prayer of Thanksgiving," or simply "The Great Thanksgiving." It has been called the prayer of consecration or dedication, emphasizing only one aspect of the prayer—the request that God may consecrate the elements, that they may be for us the body and blood of Christ. Recovering the name "eucharistic prayer" or "Great Thanksgiving" highlights the spirit of thanksgiving that marked Jesus' ministry and meals.

The eucharistic prayer is part of the sacrament variously called Holy Communion, Lord's Supper, the Eucharist, or the Mass. It follows the bringing forward of bread and cup and precedes breaking the bread and giving the bread and cup. Words, symbols, and actions, sanctified by the presence of the triune God, combine to form the sacrament. The eucharistic prayer contains the words that express the meaning of the sacrament.

Understanding the eucharistic prayer is an important part of preparation for ordained ministry. The main reason for ordination, in my view, is to provide Christian leaders who understand traditions well enough to pass them on faithfully and to reshape them to meet contemporary needs. In this way, the Christian community has an identity that is stable, yet ever in process of reformation. The prayer at table, almost always entrusted to clergy, expresses the meaning of Holy Communion and the heart of Christian praise.[1] Since those who lead the eucharistic prayer are responsible to the church of past, present, and future, they should be able to lead it with understanding and care.

The Theology of the
Eucharistic Prayer

Denominations differ in the amount of freedom in wording they offer to persons authorized to preside at communion. Some denominations, such as the Disciples of Christ, have traditionally valued locally prepared or extemporaneous prayers over prayers from books.[2] The most recent books of worship for Presbyterians and United Church of Christ members offer presiders outlines for locally prepared or extemporaneous eucharistic prayers, though full texts approved by the denomination may be used more frequently.[3] The Episcopal Church requires use of one of several approved eucharistic prayers; two options allow priests to prepare major sections of the prayer locally, on occasions other than the principal or weekly Eucharist of a parish.[4] The Roman Catholic Church has approved four basic eucharistic prayers, as well as offering, on an experimental basis, other prayers for masses of reconciliation and masses with children.[5] Through practice, though not requirement, almost all Lutherans follow their denomination's approved eucharistic prayers.[6] This chapter will serve the needs of different groups in different ways. Those who prepare their own eucharistic prayers on occasion will find guidance to do so with theological and liturgical integrity, as will persons who adapt denominational prayers. Exploring the theology and structure of the prayer may be of help also to those who are not preparing their own prayers. Many of the United Methodist students at Garrett-Evangelical Theological Seminary plan to use denominationally prepared prayers when they preside at communion. They report, however, that a class assignment to prepare or adapt a eucharistic prayer gives them a much deeper understanding of

United Methodist prayers. Deepened understanding helps presiders pray with sensitivity and care.

When Jesus prayed at the table, he blessed and thanked the God who bestows the gifts of life. Thanksgiving to God is a great theological theme that should be central in every celebration of communion. While there is much suffering and much cause for lament in human life, we give thanks because God gives us life and shares our life in Jesus Christ. We give thanks that though the power of death is strong, the power of God's love is stronger still. Holy Communion is not a funeral service (as if Jesus had died but never rose again) nor a celebration that ignores the realities of life (as if Jesus never shared our suffering). Instead, it is a meal of thanksgiving in which we give thanks for the presence of Jesus the Christ not only at table, but in our daily lives with their joy and trouble.

Jesus said, "When you do this" (celebrate communion) "remember me."[7] Remembrance of Jesus is another central theological theme of Holy Communion. Since at least the third century, the church has remembered particularly the last meal Jesus shared with his disciples before he died and his words over the bread ("This is my body") and over the cup ("This is my blood"). When theologians in the twelfth and thirteenth centuries identified the essential words for each sacrament, they identified remembrance of Jesus at the last supper as the key words ("form") necessary for Holy Communion. The churches of the Reformation included the account of the last supper in communion orders, even when rejecting other parts of the eucharistic prayer. Protestants call this account the "institution narrative," believing that it tells the story of how Jesus began ("instituted") the church's meal.

Today, while almost always retaining the institution narrative, many Christians set the last supper in the context of the whole story of Jesus Christ and the meals he shared with the outcast, the times he fed the hungry, and the meals the risen Christ shared with disciples. For example, the United Church of Christ invitation to Holy Communion begins:

> Beloved in Christ,
> the Gospel tells us that on the first day of the week
> Jesus Christ was raised from death,

appeared to Mary Magdalene,
on that same day sat at the table with two disciples,
and was made known to them in the breaking of the bread.[8]

Allen Happe, pastor of First Church in Cambridge (Massachusetts)—Congregational, United Church of Christ, has designed communion liturgies that tell the stories of Jesus' meals correlated with each season of the church year.[9] The service for Epiphany season emphasizes Jesus' feeding of the hungry, the service for Maundy Thursday recalls Jesus' last supper, and the service for Eastertide highlights the resurrection meals. Communion liturgies today generally remember not only Jesus' meals but also his incarnation, life, ministry, death, and resurrection. They speak of Jesus Christ as risen and present in the community and not simply one who lived long ago.

Openness to the transforming work of the Spirit at table and in the world is another central theme of Holy Communion. Churches understand what happens in the sacrament in varied ways. Some emphasize transformation of the elements; others emphasize transformation of those who participate; still others believe that both elements and communicants are transformed. They generally agree, however, that transformation happens not because of human words and actions alone, but because of the Spirit's work in the church and world, transforming lives and relationships. Eucharistic prayers express openness to the Spirit and ask for the fruits of the Spirit in the life and ministry of the church. Traditionally this part of the eucharistic prayer is called the *epiclesis,* a Greek word that means "invocation."[10]

Holy Communion is not simply a time when individuals, in quiet meditation, give thanks to God, remember Christ, and open themselves to the Spirit. For, as Paul writes, "Because there is one bread, we who are many are one body, for we all partake of the one bread" (1 Cor. 10:17). Those who share the meal are being formed into one community in all our diversity; this, too, is an important element of eucharistic praying.

Most eucharistic prayers include an "oblation," or offering. In Roman Catholic tradition this is an offering of the bread and cup to God, who will transform it. Martin Luther rejected this understanding, because he felt it contributed to the abuse of the Roman mass in his time. He challenged the belief that offering many masses could release souls from purgatory. He believed this belief made Christians dependent on the human works of priests, when they should depend on God's grace alone. Now that Reformation polemics have receded, however, some Protestants can speak of offering the things of ordinary life to God for blessing as an expression of trust in God's grace. Others prefer to speak of offering praise and thanksgiving, or offering themselves in commitment to God, in response to God's love, rather than of offering the bread and cup.

Finally, Holy Communion is a rehearsal of the world as God has created it to be. Jesus often describes the reign of God in parables about great banquets to which everyone, especially society's outcast, is invited. The meal is a foretaste of shared life in community where all are welcome and all share the gifts of life. This taste of God's future motivates Christians to live in a spirit of welcome, sharing, and justice.

Thanksgiving to God, remembrance of Jesus Christ, openness to the Holy Spirit, the communion of the faithful, offering, and rehearsal of God's reign are theological themes that characterize prayers at the table. These themes, in varied ways, reflect the theologies of different Christian groups. It is well to include all these themes in a eucharistic prayer. As we shall see, this can be done in a prayer that is quite brief.

The earliest eucharistic prayer that we still possess is attributed to Hippolytus, bishop of Rome, around 215–217 C.E. The prayer is offered as a model, assuming local freedom to develop eucharistic prayers. The prayer includes most of the theological themes outlined above. The headings identify parts of the prayer and will lead us into a discussion of the structure of the eucharistic prayer.

[The presider] shall give thanks, saying:

Introductory dialogue (Sursum corda)
The Lord be with you;
and all shall say:
   And with your spirit.
Up with your hearts.
   We have them with the Lord.
Let us give thanks to the Lord.

It is fitting and right.

And then [the presider] shall continue thus:

Thanksgiving (Eucharistia)
We render thanks to you, O God,
through your beloved child Jesus Christ,
whom in the last times you sent to us
a saviour and redeemer and angel of your will;
who is your inseparable Word,
through whom you made all things,
and in whom you were well pleased.
You sent him from heaven into the Virgin's womb;
and, conceived in the womb,
he was made flesh and was manifested as your Son,
being born of the holy Spirit and the Virgin.
Fulfilling your will and gaining for you a holy people,
he stretched out his hands when he should suffer,
that he might release from suffering those who have believed in
    you.

Institution narrative
And when he was betrayed to voluntary suffering
that he might destroy death,
and break the bonds of the devil,
and tread down hell, and shine upon the righteous,
and fix a term, and manifest the resurrection,
he took bread and gave thanks to you, saying,
"Take, eat; this is my body, which shall be broken for you."
Likewise also the cup, saying,
"This is my blood, which is shed for you;
when you do this, you make my remembrance."

Remembrance (anamnesis) and oblation (offering)
Remembering therefore his death and resurrection,
we offer to you the bread and the cup,
giving you thanks
because you have held us worthy to stand before you
and minister to you.

Prayer for the Holy Spirit (epiclesis)
And we ask that you would send your holy Spirit
upon the offering of your holy Church;
that, gathering (it) into one,

you would grant to all who partake of the holy things
(to partake) for the fullness of the holy Spirit
for the strengthening of faith in truth,

Doxology (closing words of praise)
that we may praise and glorify you
through your child Jesus Christ,
through whom be glory and honour to you with the holy Spirit,
in your holy Church, both now and to the ages of ages.
[And the people say:] Amen.[11]

Here is a prayer I have compiled from several modern sources,
with another theological perspective, but a similar structure:

Introductory dialogue
LEADER: God is with you.
ALL: And also with you.
LEADER: Let us open our hearts.
ALL: We open our hearts to God and one another.
LEADER: Let us give thanks.
ALL: We thank God with joy.

Thanksgiving
LEADER: "Holy God, our loving Creator, . . .
   we thank you for your constant love for all you have made."[12]
   Your breath gives us life;
   your word brings new life out of death.
   You call us from separation and sin
   to a joyful life of communion with you
   and all your creatures.
   With all people and all creation, we sing your praise:

Sanctus
ALL: "Holy, holy, holy God of love and majesty,
   the whole universe speaks of your glory,
   O God Most High.
   Blessed is the one who comes in the name of our God!
   Hosanna in the highest!"[13]

Thanksgiving continues
LEADER: Holy God, we see and touch your Word in Jesus Christ,
who communed with the outcast,
who died among sinners,
and who lives among us still.

Remembrance and offering
Remembering your boundless love for us in Jesus Christ,
we offer you our praise,
as we proclaim the mystery of faith:

Memorial acclamation
ALL: Christ has died.
   Christ has risen.
   Christ will come again.

Prayer for the Spirit
Holy God, pour your Spirit on us,
that we may know Christ in the breaking of bread,
and that in word and deed we may be channels of your love,
   peace, and justice in the world.

Concluding doxology
ALL: All praise to you, Eternal God,
   in Jesus Christ, who lives among us,
   and the Holy Spirit, who binds us together in love. Amen.

The institution narrative comes next, followed by the distribution of elements.

Theological Themes

Both prayers emphasize praise and thanksgiving, from the introductory dialogue to the concluding doxology. They remember Jesus and his institution of the supper, though in ways that are different in theology and structure. They include a prayer for the Holy Spirit. Hippolytus's prayer (like many eucharistic prayers, but unlike mine) asks God to send the Spirit on the offering (bread and wine); my prayer asks God to send the Spirit that we may know Christ in the breaking of bread (Luke 24:35) and that we may be channels of God's reign on earth. The element of rehearsal that occurs in my prayer is less evident in the prayer of Hippolytus. Hippolytus speaks of offering the bread and the cup; I speak of offering praise. Both prayers emphasize the communal nature of the sacrament, not only through words but through the congregation's participation in prayer. Although an ordained presider may speak the eucharistic prayer, congregational responses affirm that everyone is praying silently.[14]

The Structure of the
Eucharistic Prayer

Having noted the theological themes usually present in the eucharistic prayer, we can consider its structure. The prayer itself is part of a larger structure that follows an order from several passages in Luke and Acts (Luke 9:16; Luke 22:19; Luke 24:30; Acts 27:35): taking the bread and the cup, blessing them, breaking the bread, and giving the elements. The prayer is the blessing.

Here is a typical order for the eucharistic prayer:

Invitation
Introductory dialogue
Opening thanksgiving
Seasonal preface
Sanctus
Thanksgiving continues
Institution narrative
Remembrance and offering
Memorial acclamation
Prayer for the Holy Spirit and for the fruits of the Spirit
Concluding doxology
Amen.

Let us consider each part in turn.

The Invitation

The invitation welcomes the people, in the name of Jesus Christ, to partake of communion, usually giving some sense of the breadth of the invitation (all Christians? all people? all who seek to live in love with their neighbors?). Here is an opportunity to express the all-encompassing nature of the gospel.

The Introductory Dialogue

The introductory dialogue (often called the *sursum corda*, which in Latin means "up with your hearts") asks the people to join the presider in praying. It corresponds to the informal dialogue in evangelical tradition when a leader asks, "Are you praying with me?" and everyone responds, "Yes!" The version in the ancient prayer is much more typical than the second prayer, which is adapted for theological reasons. The couplet "God is with you"— "And also with you" uses "God" as a less gender-specific name than "Lord," and it affirms that God is always with us (even when we are not present to God). The words, "Open your hearts," and "We open them to God and to one another," come from a eucharistic order by Carter Heyward.[15] This wording is excellent because it expresses openness to God without using images from a three-storied universe where God lives "up there"; it also points to the communal nature of the sacrament. The last couplet reflects my discomfort with the way some prayers imply that we give thanks to God out of duty; for prayer is a privilege and joy as well as a responsibility for Christians.

Opening Thanksgiving and Sanctus

Words of thanksgiving come next, and the two examples demonstrate two traditions. Hippolytus immediately moves into thanksgiving for Jesus Christ, as do many prayers, usually punctuating the thanksgiving with the Sanctus in the middle. My prayer follows another common tradition of giving thanks for God's work in all time and all creation before the Sanctus, then following it with thanks for what God has done in Jesus Christ. The Sanctus is an ancient response to the opening thanksgiving. It takes its name from the Latin word for "holy," with which it begins. The Sanctus is found in most eucharistic prayers today.

Still another tradition is to include a "preface" that varies with seasons and occasions of the church year immediately before the Sanctus.

Institution Narrative

Most eucharistic prayers, like that of Hippolytus's, move from thanksgiving for Christ into telling the institution narrative. My prayer, however, follows the Reformed tradition of keeping the narrative outside the prayer. In that tradition the narrative commonly is placed with the invitation as a "warrant," a way of explaining why communion is celebrated. Here I follow the alternative tradition (practiced widely in the United Church of Christ, a church of Reformed heritage) in which the institution narrative follows the prayer.

The movement from praying to telling the institution narrative in most eucharistic prayers often marks a subtle shift from speaking to God to speaking to the congregation. I prefer to follow the U.S. Congregationalist practice of telling the narrative after the prayer and before the distribution of the elements. The institution, if included in the prayer, must be carefully integrated into the prayer. Many prayers adapt the narrative to a prayer form, as Hippolytus did, by adding "to you" where the scripture passage says, "he gave thanks" ("he took bread and gave thanks *to you*.)" This helpfully weaves the story into prayer. I also appreciate the brevity of Hippolytus's account, which helps maintain the tone of prayer. Quoting the full scripture narrative can make it seem that the presider is speaking to the congregation, not God, especially when the prayer also includes many narrative details about Jesus. Some literature about worship today speaks approvingly of this narrative quality of the eucharistic prayer, as a way of recounting all God's mighty acts. This approach risks turning the prayer into a sermon. Wherever the institution narrative is located, eucharistic prayers should avoid crossing the thin line between giving thanks to God and telling stories to the congregation. The eucharistic prayer should express the height and depth of our thanksgiving and praise to God, complementing the sermon, without being another sermon.

Remembrance and Offering

The whole section of the prayer that speaks of Jesus Christ is sometimes called the remembrance (or *anamnesis*); this does not, however, refer to reflection on the past so much as representation of the past and the living presence of Christ. More technically, the anamnesis follows the institution narrative, typically begins with the word "remembering" (in English language liturgies), and describes the church's self-offering in response to Christ.

Offering appropriately follows remembrance. Remembering what God has done in Christ calls for a response, an offering of the bread and the cup, of praise and thanksgiving, or of our very selves.

Memorial Acclamation

The memorial acclamation that follows the offering is a welcome modern addition to ancient tradition; through it, the congregation (not only the presider) remembers the whole work of Christ.

Prayer for the Holy Spirit and the
Fruit of the Spirit

In approaching the table—toward the end of the prayer—Christians invoke the Holy Spirit. (In some traditions prayer for the Spirit appears earlier in the prayer as well.) This part of the prayer often leads into an anticipation of the fruits of the Spirit. The wording varies according to the theology of the church or church leader composing the prayer.

Concluding Doxology

The eucharistic prayer closes as it begins, by giving thanks and praise to God. Usually the concluding doxology is trinitarian in form. It is interesting to note that, though some modern liturgical scholars believe the prayer should begin and end with a reference to God as Father, the prayer of Hippolytus expresses trinitarian faith without doing so.

Amen

The unison "amen" at the end expresses the people's consent and participation in the prayer. Justin Martyr describes the eucharistic prayer in Rome about the year 155 c.e.:

> Bread is brought, and wine and water, and the president similarly sends up prayers and thanksgiving to the best of his ability, and the congregation assents, saying the Amen; the distribution, and reception of the consecrated [elements] by each one, takes place and they are sent to the absent by the deacons.[16]

As Justin says, "Amen" is a response of assent by the congregation to what the presider has said. It literally means, "So be it," in Hebrew. The "amen" should not be taken for granted or usurped by clergy; it is an important part of the eucharistic prayer. (Note also that Justin assumes that presiders will prepare prayers locally "to the best of [their] ability" and that thanksgiving will be central in the prayer.)

Many churches follow the distribution of communion with a "prayer after communion." The typical themes of such prayers are thanksgiving for the presence of Christ at the table and a request for the gifts of the Spirit for the life and ministry of the church. Since the eucharistic prayer ordinarily includes these themes, a hymn and final blessing and charge may be just as appropriate following communion.

Form and Creativity

Even within the classic structure of the eucharistic prayer outlined in the last section, there are many variations, as even two examples show. *The United Methodist Book of Worship* includes five general eucharistic prayers, twelve versions of the Great Thanksgiving for use at different times in the church year, plus a version for use at services of Christian marriage and at services of death and resurrection.[17] Janet Morley has developed several eucharistic prayers that have a feminist perspective and are based on the classic structure.[18] The Sanctus, the memorial acclamation, and the amen are sung to a multitude of settings; some churches have sung other words in response. Variation within the classic structure is endless, both in church history and in present liturgical resources. The eucharistic prayer is a good example of structure that can channel and discipline our creativity.

The free churches have adopted the classic structure much later than more liturgical churches, if at all; and free churches that have offered classic liturgies cannot mandate their use. Those who prefer a much simpler form of eucharistic prayer would do well, however, to incorporate the time-honored theological themes of thanksgiving, remembrance, institution narrative, offering, invocation of the Spirit, and rehearsal of God's reign. These themes can be incorporated into extemporaneous prayer, if the presider thoroughly understands the structure and theology of the eucharistic prayer. I provide the following example as a way to incorporate a fuller theology of Holy Communion in a brief prayer:

> We praise you, loving God, for creating all things,
> for making us in your image,
> and for seeking us when we turn from you.

We thank you for coming to us in Jesus Christ,
who was faithful even to death on the cross
and who lives among us still.
We share this meal in remembrance of him,
offering you our lives in praise and thanksgiving.
Fill us with your Spirit, to make us one in Christ,
and one in love for you and for all people,
as in word and deed we seek your reign of peace and justice
on earth.
Glory be to you, eternal God, through Jesus Christ,
in the power of the Holy Spirit. Amen.[19]

The story of the Last Supper would be told in narrative form outside the prayer. Congregations can learn to say the "Amen" after the closing doxology and a few seconds of silence; they could participate in the prayer by singing a favorite song or by standing in a circle around the presider.

The church's tradition of prayer at the table is far richer than these few pages can describe. Given the great diversity of forms, the two most important things in composing a eucharistic prayer are to include the key theological themes for Holy Communion and to offer ways for the congregation to take part in the prayer. No words are adequate to give thanks to the God of Jesus Christ, but by calling on our deepest creative selves and learning from the richest historical traditions, we can do our best to find words for the Great Thanksgiving.

8

Finding Words
to Sing

Hymns, because they combine words and music and actively engage most of the congregation, are central to worship. In some Protestant churches that give congregations few words to speak, hymns form most of the people's active worship. Hymns cling to the memory through rhyme, rhythm, and melody. A snatch of a hymn can run through a Christian's mind in the midst of routine daily work, a reminder of God's presence. In a time of pain or crisis, a hymn provides comfort or challenge. Then, returning to church on Sunday, members sing with renewed enthusiasm hymns that may have sustained them through the week.

Hymns serve many theological purposes. Many hymns express praise to God. Others petition God for wisdom, strength, or courage; still others pour out honest lament. The great majority of hymns address God directly. Through them, the congregation forms and renews its relationship with God. Some speak in singular voice; for example, "Lord, I Want to Be a Christian," appropriately expresses the commitment of each individual in community. Since hymns are meant for congregational singing, many speak in plural about shared life experiences. For instance, Charles Albert Tindley (1851–1933), an African American Methodist pastor, helped urban Christians express to God their common experience in a hymn that begins: "We are tossed and driven on the restless seas of time."[1] Even hymns in singular voice, however, are sung together; hymns are never purely individualistic, though they may focus on individual faith experience.

Some hymns, such as "A Mighty Fortress Is Our God" by

Martin Luther (1483–1546), address not God but humanity. Their theological purpose may be to proclaim who God is, to tell what God does, or to challenge Christians to faithfulness. Not a few begin by witnessing to humanity and end by addressing God; the first stanza of "Lift Every Voice and Sing" asks humans to sing of hope and liberty, while the third stanza addresses God directly.[2]

Hymns express and shape our faith not only through their words but also through their music. Church leaders through the centuries have feared that singers, enchanted by a delightful tune, might miss the meaning of words. Yet texts and tunes can weave together in such a way that the music intensifies meaning. Consider the contrast between the tunes *Passion Chorale,* sung on Good Friday with the text "O Sacred Head Now Wounded," and *Easter Hymn,* sung with the text "Christ the Lord Is Risen Today" on Easter morning. If it were possible to exchange the texts, how poorly the tunes would express the sorrow of Good Friday or the joy of Easter! Tunes are part of the meaning hymns express.

Hymns give voice to faith in cultural forms through the style of both music and words. Singing their faith in the characteristic musical forms of a culture can help people sing more wholeheartedly with a greater depth of feeling. This is true of national and ethnic cultures as well as regional and class subcultures. One congregation listens to country music, another attends classical concerts; different hymns will inspire them. Diverse styles of hymns help diverse congregations express their faith. Worshiping the living God demands the very best forms of the culture or cultures of a worshiping community.

Hymns communicate faith as congregations sing to or about God. Words and music, in forms growing out of human cultures, support one another to convey meaning and join people in a common voice. Hymns are inherently collective; they express the faith of the community singing together. They help a congregation participate actively in worship.

Selecting Hymns

Those who choose hymns for worship have an awesome task— helping people express and grow in their relationship with God and

Christian discipleship. Personal preference, theological training, or aesthetic sensitivity may guide the selection of hymns for congregational singing, but concern for the worship and faith development of communities who sing is also essential.

Concern for the overall integration of worship means that hymns should relate to the themes and scripture texts for the service. This requires that worship planners read the entire hymn text to discover if it is truly appropriate. More than one worship planner has been startled to find that a hymn text develops in a direction not anticipated by the opening line; one phrase that fits the direction of the service is not enough. Consistency in the overall direction of hymn and the overall direction of the service is the goal. Sometimes connections are subtle, but the themes of hymns and worship should not be inconsistent.

Concern for worship means that the words of a hymn should be appropriate to the part of a service in which it appears. Almost any act of worship can be sung, from opening words to prayers to closing blessings. Hymns then should be placed where they belong in the order of service. It is always appropriate to begin worship by praising God in song; a hymn can carry the same content as a call to worship or greeting. The hymn closest to the scripture readings and sermons should be closely related to the directions being explored in preaching. Appropriately worded hymns and congregational responses enhance celebrations of the sacrament. Hymns toward the end of the service anticipate a congregation's going into the world to love God and humanity. A hymn should never interrupt, but rather always continue, the progression of the service in both content and emotional mood.

Obviously, not only words but also tunes convey the meanings and moods of worship, supporting or subverting the progression of a service. An Advent hymn tune might voice expectation; a Lenten hymn tune might articulate the enthusiasm of baptismal commitment or the grief of the cross. A lively hymn of praise might support worship that has a joyful theme, but it might begin a more contemplative service on the wrong note.

Finding hymn texts that fit the themes, texts, and progression of worship requires effort. The scripture and subject indexes of a hymnal can aid the search for appropriate hymns. If a scripture con-cordance supplement has been published for the hymnal a congre-gation uses, it will provide more detailed help. Churches that follow the lectionary and/or church year often will find appropriate hymns in sections of the hymnal or the section of a hymnal index catego-rized by the church year. Planners can save time by choosing the hymns for a whole season at one sitting. Planning ahead also makes it possible for musicians to prepare preludes or postludes based on one of the hymns for the day.

The task would be forbidding enough if worship planners only needed to consider how the words and tunes of hymns fit into wor-ship. But concern for the congregation's heartfelt participation and their faith development places another set of challenges before the worship planner.

Heartfelt participation is possible when the choice of hymns in a service balances familiarity and challenge. New hymns with chal-lenging tunes need careful introduction, perhaps the first time as an anthem by the choir. For example, the text "Hope of the World," by theologian Georgia Harkness (1891–1974), was perfect for a service I was planning for a church I had just begun serving as interim pas-tor. Unfortunately, the congregation had never sung the hymn, which was set in their hymnal to a difficult tune they did not know. I had not sought ways to introduce the hymn that would help the congregation become familiar with it, and they rebelled: "Don't *ever* choose that hymn again!"

In general, though, the same congregation would accept one less familiar hymn per service, if they could also sing familiar hymns. The issue at stake is whether worshipers must devote most of their attention to learning new things or whether they have the oppor-tunity to forget themselves and their performance in the act of prais-ing God. Like many congregations who object to unfamiliar hymns, they were not clinging to the past, but insisting that I allow them to participate fully in worship.

One man in the same congregation told me privately after a service, "I wish you would introduce us to more new hymns. Singing the same hymns all the time makes worship less interesting to me." Of course, I was delighted with the support of this adventuresome member, who was reminding me that fresh hymnody also supports participation in worship. Some worshipers thrive on novelty; too much repetition becomes boring or trite to them. Learning new hymns can help a congregation grow, as people discover new ways to articulate their faith. For most people, gentle and gradual learning, rather than a rush of new material, supports heartfelt participation and spiritual development. Many excellent methods have helped congregations learn new hymns gradually but systematically. The book *Hymns and Their Uses* by James Sydnor outlines a number of them.[3]

Another consideration in choosing hymns is the cultural tradition or diversity of a congregation. Clergy and musicians who come from a different region, class, or denomination than the congregations they serve need humility when choosing hymns, in order to be open to member's preferences rather than to impose supposedly universal aesthetic standards. Some very gifted people dismiss whole categories of hymnody as inferior without taking time to learn about them. Closer study will reveal that hymns of each type—from classical to folk to gospel to contemporary Christian—range greatly in appropriateness for congregational singing.

Accessibility of words and music was the key purpose of evangelical gospel hymns—but that does not mean that profound theological insights and sound composition cannot be found among them. Excellence in composition and poetry has characterized much classical hymnody of the past and present, but not every well-written classical hymn is accessible for congregational singing. Some folk hymns (especially those composed in the 1960s and 1970s) are shapeless melodically, but others are haunting in their simple but engaging form. Similarly, some praise choruses that have become popular recently have engaging, accessible texts and tunes, though they may not be nourishing as the only diet for hymnody.[4] The litany could go on—each musical style offers both riches and pitfalls for congregational song. Worship leaders should listen carefully, therefore, to what congregations prefer singing, seeking sound theology and composition, yet open to the styles the congregation loves. Abstract standards for correct church music lead to insensitivity about local culture. When church leaders combine good training with compassionate listening, they can help congregations broaden their musical tastes without abandoning the hymnody they have come to love. The goal in most congregations should be to incorporate a more diverse hymnody, honoring hymns already loved, while learning new hymns of other styles and cultures. In this way, congregations make room for diversity within the present congregation and among the new members who may join with them in praising and serving God.

Writing New Hymn Texts

The remaining material in this chapter is designed especially for writers of original hymn texts; more technical than most material in the book, it still may help people choose or evaluate hymns. Moreover, almost any hymn-singing Christian might well attempt to write an original hymn once in a lifetime. Some may uncover a hidden gift or a new spiritual discipline. All will gain a new appreciation of hymn text writing, which demands all the discipline and creativity one can muster.

What motivation could one possibly have to write a hymn text, when hundreds of thousands already exist in one's native tongue and when congregations love to sing familiar songs? There are three main reasons: (1) to express the writer's religious devotion; (2) to address a topic not yet addressed in traditional hymnody; or (3) to explore a familiar topic in a new way.

Good hymnody overflows from living a relationship with God. Composer and educator Austin Lovelace argues that the best hymns happen when a person is so full of the love of God that one has no choice but to write hymns, using well-trained gifts: "Great hymns can be created only when poetic gifts and techniques are so developed that God's Spirit can flow through the mind, heart, and hand of a poet-Christian who must sing of God's grace."[5] While some keep journals, others write hymns as a spiritual discipline and later share them in or beyond their worshiping congregation.[6] Other hymns arise spontaneously in a crisis; Scottish poet and pastor George Matheson (1842–1906) wrote "O Love That Wilt Not Let Me Go" while in great pain. He said this of its writing:

> It was composed with extreme rapidity; it seemed to me that its con-
> struction occupied only a few minutes, and I felt myself rather in the
> position of one who was being dictated to than of an original artist. I
> was suffering from extreme mental stress and the hymn was the fruit
> of that pain.[7]

The hymn text, God's gift for Matheson's healing, has assured many
others that divine love embraces them and leads them past grief.
This, then, is the first purpose for writing a hymn: to express one's
faith and give others the words to express their faith.

A second reason to write hymns is to fill a need in worship not
met by hymns readily available. Growing attention to the lectionary
and church year has created a void in hymnody. For example, until
recently few Protestant churches in the United States celebrated
Epiphany. The feast, observed on January 6, celebrates the manifestation of Jesus as the Christ and Word of God through the incarnation, the visitation of the Magi, his baptism by John, and other
events early in Jesus' ministry. Churches and hymnal committees
have sought hymns for the occasion, since the few good traditional
Epiphany hymns emphasize only the coming of the Magi. Now that
many denominations use the same lectionary, hymn texts that bring
out the themes and images of a particular Sunday meet a need.

The churches' new awareness of areas of ministry and justice
calls for new hymns. A hymn I wrote about the church's ministry of
healing with persons suffering the wounds of abuse serves a need in
healing services and twelve-step groups, among other settings. Hymns
of confession, hope, and healing are needed to respond to growing
awareness of how humanity is ravaging nature. As the church begins to value women's contributions, hymn-poets tell the stories of
women in scripture, church history, and contemporary society.
These are just a few topics that rarely have been addressed but that
now inspire many new hymn texts.

A third reason to write a hymn text is to sing about a familiar
subject in a new way. Psalm 19 proclaims God's work in nature; it
has inspired hymns that reflect understandings of creation in various historical periods. Hymn writers play an important role in re-
shaping inherited ideas and images so that their contemporaries can
sing their faith honestly.[8]

Deep experiences of faith and life, unexplored subject matter, and fresh ways of approaching familiar subjects can inspire fresh and useful new hymn texts. Unfortunately, many beginning hymn writers imitate the past, repeating ideas and rearranging phrases of other poets, without trying to uncover what is urging toward expression today. A facility at rhyme and meter is not enough for good hymnwriting; writers also must have something to say that has not been said before in the same way.

Finding the creative voice is of utmost importance in hymnody. Hymns follow a highly structured form, yet their content expresses the love, hope, fear, commitment, and longing of Christians. To be a fitting expression of a congregation's relationship with God, hymn texts must touch the heart and the imagination, melding with music to express praise, lament, thanksgiving, and prayer. No hymn writer can predict what texts will help others express their relationship with God, but a text seldom will speak to others unless it honestly grows out of one's journey with God. Nowhere is beginning in prayer and tapping the imagination more important than with hymn writing, given the many hymns readily available for people to sing.

The creative voice must speak at the depth of a hymn text, however, and not on the surface. A movie I saw recently was flawed by showy camera work that constantly called attention to itself, as if to say, "Isn't this original?" The filmmaker's cleverness distracted from the development of the plot and characters. This kind of originality also is distracting in hymn texts. True originality comes from honest expression of one's perceptions of life and faith. Julia Cameron, whose book *The Artist's Way* has helped many people recover their creative selves, has written "It is the accurate mapping out of our own creative interests that invites the term *original*. We are the *origin* of our art, its homeland. Viewed this way, originality is the process of remaining true to ourselves."[9]

In a hymn that is "original," each word says something one wants to say; nothing is "filler." Originality grows not simply out of individual experience but from a writer's immersion in the life of the church and the world. Originality in hymns is, to a large extent, a matter of context—speaking out of a particular time, place, and community. African American spirituals speak from an oppressive and life-denying context, melding imagery, musical forms, and confident Christian witness in a unique way. Yet, rooted in a particular context, these hymns speak to Christians around the world, because they express honestly what it means for Christians to affirm life in the face of oppression and death.

The reason to write a hymn text is to express what must be expressed out of our lives and contexts. Otherwise, we will certainly repeat the past. Originality comes as we allow the Spirit of creation to speak through us from within our contexts.

Disciplines of
Hymn Text Writing

Writing hymn texts requires disciplines beyond those already discussed because of the challenge of helping congregations sing. Interesting, regular patterns of rhythm and rhyme enable people to sing together. Using rhythm and rhyme is a craft that can be learned, yet which is time-consuming to do well.

The Rhythm of Hymns

In the back of every hymnal is a metrical index, grouping hymns by their rhythm patterns. In this system, "Love Divine, All Loves Excelling" by Charles Wesley (1707–1788) is listed as 8.7.8.7.D. ("D" means "doubled"; so 8.7.8.7.D. means 8.7.8.7. doubled.) If you are unfamiliar with the system, count the syllables in each line of one stanza of "Love Divine" (see illustration 1). You will discover the first line has eight syllables, and the second line has seven. This pattern is repeated four times. Now find another tune your hymnal lists as 8.7.8.7.D.; you can probably sing "Love Divine" to it.

Several abbreviations in metrical indexes bear explanation; they refer to a few meters that English language hymnody often uses. Common Meter (C.M.) is 8.6.8.6.; an example is ST. ANNE, often sung with "O God, Our Help in Ages Past." C.M.D., which means Common Meter Doubled, is also a popular meter. Short Meter (S.M.) is 6.6.8.6.; an example is DENNIS, often sung with "Blest Be the Tie That Binds." Long Meter (L.M.), often used in early hymns, especially ancient Latin hymns, is 8.8.8.8., exemplified by OLD

Love Divine, All Loves Excelling

HYFRYDOL 8.7.8.7 D

Charles Wesley, 1747

Rowland Hugh Prichard, 1831

1. Love di - vine, all loves ex - cel - ling, Joy of heaven, to
2. Breathe, O breathe Thy lov - ing Spir - it In - to ev - ery
3. Come, Al - might - y to de - liv - er, Let us all Thy
4. Fin - ish, then, Thy new cre - a - tion; Pure and spot - less

earth come down, Fix in us Thy hum - ble dwell - ing,
trou - bled breast! Let us all in Thee in - her - it,
life re - ceive; Sud - den - ly re - turn, and nev - er,
let us be; Let us see Thy great sal - va - tion

All Thy faith - ful mer - cies crown! Je - sus, Thou art all com -
Let us find the prom - ised rest; Take a - way the love of
Nev - er - more Thy tem - ples leave. Thee we would be al - ways
Per - fect - ly re - stored in Thee; Changed from glo - ry in - to

pas - sion, Pure, un - bound - ed love Thou art; Vis - it us with
sin - ning; Al - pha and O - me - ga be; End of faith, as
bless - ing, Serve Thee as Thy hosts a - bove; Pray, and praise Thee
glo - ry, Till in heaven we take our place, Till we cast our

Thy sal - va - tion, En - ter ev - ery trem - bling heart.
its be - gin - ning, Set our hearts at lib - er - ty.
with - out ceas - ing, Glo - ry in Thy per - fect love.
crowns be - fore Thee, Lost in won - der, love, and praise.

Reproduced from *The Presbyterian Hymnal: Hymns, Psalms and Spiritual Songs.*
©1990 Westminister/John Knox Press.

100th, best known as a tune for the Doxology. Hymn tune names are always listed in all capital letters.

Since hymnals contain hymns translated from many languages, indexes list many other meters, some ill-suited to English language rhythms. Yet text writers today often are encouraged to venture into writing in a greater variety of meters, making it possible for composers to compose fresh new tunes. The metrical index can help worship leaders find a familiar tune that will encourage a congregation to sing a new text. It also can help writers identify good tunes for their texts.

Caution is in order. Some tunes convey the wrong feeling for some texts. Further, a congregation must know a tune by memory to sing it to a new text, unless the tune is very easy to learn. It is not wise to ask a congregation to hold a new text in one hand and a hymnal with the tune set with a different text in the other hand! Third, not only the number of syllables but their rhythm must be considered.

The basic building block of rhythm in English language poetry is a "foot," the smallest unit of poetic rhythm: an accented syllable together with one or more unaccented syllables. Four kinds of feet are common in English-language hymn texts: the iamb, the trochee, the anapest, and the dactyl. Iambic feet are feet of two syllables with the second accented: diVINE. Trochaic feet have two syllables with the first accented: WORship. An anapestic foot has three syllables with the third accented: in the NIGHT. A dactylic foot has three syllables with the first accented: CARoling. Lines with the same number of syllables may rely on different kinds of poetic feet. Hymnal indexes list 8.7.8.7. trochaic and 8.7.8.7. iambic separately because iambic and trochaic texts cannot be sung to the same tune. But not even all hymn tunes listed together are truly interchangeable. Variations in tune structure or feeling tone can make a text/tune match awkward or ridiculous; a congregation should never be asked to sing a match that planners have not first tested by singing.

Hymn text writers should attend not only to the number of syllables or the kind of poetic feet but to the contours of tunes. The strongest emphases of text and tune should match. Ordinarily, the first sounded note in a measure is stressed more than other notes.[10]

Words also receive emphasis when sung on longer or higher notes. A verb, noun, or vivid adjective would be more fitting on a long, high note than a word like "in" or "and." In turn, "in" or "and" would be more fitting on an offbeat (not the first beat of a measure), a shorter note, or perhaps a lower note. Also, words with open vowels are better on notes held a long time; they are more melodious and are easier for singers to hold without breathing. Further, one syllable of a hymn text is often sung on more than one note. Recently I wrote a text to the tune PICCARDY, usually matched with "Let All Mortal Flesh Keep Silence." In the next to the last line, one syllable is sung on four notes. An open vowel sound such as "way" sounds better than a closed sound like "van." It was challenging to find words with open vowels on that measure, but anything else was awkward to sing. Singing the words frequently while writing a hymn text helps match the text and tune.

Following the contours of a tune should not, however, lead text writers away from adhering closely to their chosen rhythm pattern. The place in PICCARDY where one syllable is sung to four notes might tempt a beginning writer to "cheat" on meter, slipping in a two-syllable word instead. Or the writer may notice that the rhythm of "Be Thou My Vision" varies once in the third stanza; the flowing folk rhythm permits "own heart" to be sung on the same two notes that carried "thought" and "on-" in earlier stanzas. The temptation is to vary meter in several places, willy-nilly, making it impossible for the singer to predict how the words will fit the tune. Once a rhythmic pattern has been established, the singer expects it to continue. When a text is set to a familiar tune, the singer expects the new text to have the same rhythm as the well-known text. Deviations in rhythm make a song more difficult to sing; they should be made infrequently if at all. Folk traditions with varied rhythms depend on outstanding song leaders to help congregations follow.

To fit well with a tune, a hymn text should have a similar structure from stanza to stanza. In a poem that would not be sung, one might state something hopeful in the first eight lines, then express an awful challenge in the next eight lines, then resolve to a larger hope in the last eight lines. But consider what a challenge this poses to the composer. How can the same tune express mild hope in one stanza, fear in the second, and strong hope in the third? Thus, the contrast between hope and threat must be structured into each stanza of a hymn text. Contrast and movement must be structured into each stanza, with the climax of the text matching the climax of the tune.

Slight variations in the rhythmic pattern can make a hymn more interesting. For example, "All People That on Earth Do Dwell" is basically iambic tetrameter (L.M.), but hymn writer and English teacher Gracia Grindal scans it this way:

ALL PEOP/le/THAT/on EARTH/do DWELL,
SING TO/the LORD/with CHEER/ful VOICE;
HIM SERVE/with MIRTH,/his PRAISE/forth TELL;
COME ye/beFORE/him AND/reJOICE.[11]

Beginning each line with a strong word varies the meter effectively, if OLD HUNDREDTH is sung with long notes at the beginning of each line. Gracia Grindal writes: "While almost anybody can write poetry which is endlessly regular, it takes the ear of the poet to hear when the line should be varied."[12] After reviewing many hymns by beginning writers, however, I would advise beginners to err on the side of regularity, starting with tunes that demand regular rhythm. After developing competent craft, the author may venture to vary rhythm to create interest or to include words one must say. Meticulous rhythm is essential to good hymn-text writing.

The Challenge of Rhyme

Hymns often rhyme. Clement Wood, compiler of a standard rhyming dictionary, has written that "Rhyme is the identity in sound of an accented vowel in a word, usually the last one accented, and of all consonantal and vowel sounds following it; with a difference in the sound of the consonant immediately preceding the accented vowel."[13] Notice the rhymes in stanza 1 of "Love Divine." The rhyming words at the end of eight-beat lines are two-syllable rhymes: "excelling" and "dwelling"; "compassion" and "salvation." The rhyming words at the ends of seven-beat lines are one-syllable rhymes: down/crown, art/heart. The 8.7.8.7.D. meter leads to this pattern, since its poetry is basically iambic, yet all the lines of seven syllables end on a single accented beat. Wesley's rhyme pattern in each stanza is ababcdcd; that is, the first and third, second and fourth, fifth and seventh, and sixth and eighth lines rhyme. In each stanza, at least one rhyme is imperfect, for example, "compassion" and "salvation" in the first stanza. Nevertheless, Wesley's rhymes give a sense of completion to the lines, which is one purpose of rhyming in hymnody. It is particularly important to end a hymn on a true rhyme to give a sense of completion.

Hymn texts often employ near rhymes of consonance and assonance. "Compassion/salvation" demonstrates consonance, since ending consonants, but not vowels, rhyme. Wesley ends "Love Divine" with assonance ("place/praise"), not a true rhyme; only the vowels rhyme, though the consonants nearly rhyme. Although Wood declares that "rhyme deals exclusively with sounds, and has nothing to do with spelling,"[14] visual rhymes (in which words such as "move/love" end with the same letters, *pronounced* differently) are not unusual in hymn texts. Hymn text writers sometimes only rhyme alternate lines, for example, rhyming only the seven-beat lines with HYFRYDOL, so that the pattern could be diagrammed: xaxaxbxb (with x representing an unrhymed line).

Rhyme is not generally in favor in secular poetry today, and not everyone agrees that rhyme is important in hymn writing. Lovelace encourages exact rhyming in every line,[15] whereas Grindal prefers near rhymes to trite ones. Recent hymn texts sometimes rhyme minimally (through assonance, consonance, visual rhymes, or infrequent rhymes), if at all.

The most important discipline of rhyming, given these many options, is to use great care in word choice, never using one word simply to rhyme with another. It is better to not rhyme or to use near rhymes than to use trite rhymes that do not really say what one wants to say. Wood lists some hackneyed rhymes:

> kiss, bliss.
> yearn, burn; yearning, burning.
> love, dove, above.
> fire, desire.
> trees, breeze.[16]

Except for "kiss/bliss," these rhymes appear fairly frequently in hymns, perhaps showing that some things too trite to say can be sung. Still, the text writer should seek varied, interesting rhymes. Rhyming should never lead to archaisms, such as using "trod" to rhyme with "God," or "unfurled" to rhyme with "world." Rhyming words should stay within the rhetoric or literary tone of the text, or the effect will be ridiculous:

> All praise to our almighty God
> who loves us whether straight or mod.[17]

Singers should not be able to guess which rhyming word was chosen first; each rhyming word should be essential to the meaning.

Hymn text writing requires the greatest discipline so that rhythm and rhyme support, rather than subvert, the writer's purpose. Thus, a rough draft may consume only a few minutes, but a finished hymn text may require at least four or five hours at several sittings to be worthy of congregational song. Sloppy word choice distracts the singer from communicating the heart's faith and praise. The goal is not poetic eloquence for its own sake, but words so natural and true that they convey the religious conviction of the singer.

Poetic Devices

Hymn writers use poetic devices such as alliteration, assonance, and imagery. Alliteration is the use of several adjacent or close-by words that begin with the same consonant. Assonance, the use of similar sounds, especially vowels, is used not only to rhyme but to enhance the sound within a line. Hymn writers use imagery most of all; they speak by word-pictures such as metaphors, similes, and descriptions of narrative or sense reality. These and other poetic devices either enhance the quality of sound or call on the imagination to express the experience of faith.

Address is part of the poetry of hymns. For example, a hymn may use personification, addressing the cross as if it were a person. Some texts, such as the last four stanzas of "How Firm a Foundation," speak in the voice of God. Hymns most commonly address God or humanity, as noted above. Others first speak to humanity, then God, requiring the writer to take care with transitions. Whoever is addressed, the hymn writer should remember that the task is to help people voice their religious experience; hymns that are, in fact, sermons are not easily used in worship. Most hymns should express the believer's relationship with God, either as a direct address to God (in praise, prayer, or lament) or as a witness to the community.

The Tools of Hymn Text Writing

Beyond computer or pencil and paper (or anything that allows for much editing), other tools are invaluable for hymn writing. A rhyming dictionary saves time and can locate an elusive rhyme. A thesaurus identifies words that convey one's intended meaning, yet fit the rhyme and rhythm scheme. A Bible grounds texts in the church's common language. A collection of hymnals offers a great variety of tunes to fit the mood and meter of texts. Such tools support disciplined hymn text writing.

Hymn Text Writing:
One Writer's Process

People are often curious how someone moves from an idea to a completed hymn text. Writers proceed in a variety of ways, so here I can describe only my process.

The idea for a hymn comes in several ways. A friend or a church will ask me to write a hymn for a special occasion. At other times, my life experiences spark ideas. Sometimes a tune will move me to write a text and suggest its subject matter. Usually I spend some time brainstorming and focusing.

My next movement toward writing a hymn text is to make a rough draft of what I want to say, perhaps including a central image. Except when a tune has inspired the text, I must then choose a rhythm in one of several ways. I may follow the rhythm of the first line, if it is well developed. Or, since some rhythms dance, some mourn, and others are stately and dignified, the feeling of the text may suggest a meter; then I search for a tune of that meter.[18] At other times, the words may remind me of an existing tune or a new tune. When I create text and tune together, I move back and forth between text and tune several times to find a regular rhythm to support congregational singing.

I prefer always to use rhyme in a hymn, perhaps only in every other line; I strive toward true rhymes. It is worth reworking or discarding a line, though not one's ideas, so that every rhyming word matters.

I usually spend two or three hours in the first composition of a text, singing each stanza several times to check the rhythm. Later, I spend considerable time revising it at separate sittings. Feedback from other writers or from the first people who sing the hymn helps me identify problems to correct.[19]

Summary

It is an awesome thing to write or select words that Christians will sing to God, for singing involves words and music, and it calls forth thoughts and feelings, memories and hopes. Writing or choosing hymns demands one's very best, for hymns are a vehicle for Christian praise, prayer, lament, commitment, and witness. When well-matched with a tune, words find wings as body, heart, mind, and soul unite in responding to God's grace.

9

Bringing It All Together

Integrating the parts of worship involves both aesthetic sensibility and disciplined creativity.

One service I attended was based around the story of Jesus' encounter with the Samaritan woman at the well in John 4. As they entered the sanctuary, worshipers already began to focus on the theme through bulletins that interpreted the story visually. Following a brief call to worship and hymn, the scripture was read dramatically by a narrator and other persons who read the parts of Jesus, the woman, and the disciples. Scripture was then interpreted by two dancers using the visual symbols of a water pitcher, the baptismal font, and abundantly rippling water. The baptismal font was the visual center of both the dance and the scripture reading. Following this proclamation through dance, a choir sang an anthem using vivid water images, accompanied by a rain stick, a South American instrument that makes the sound of rushing water. Next, the congregation members renewed their baptisms with water from pitchers filled at the font, while the choir sang "Living Water," a song by Miriam Therese Winter. The last hymn, "Freely, Freely," sent us out with an encouragement to witness to our faith in Christ as the woman at the well had done.

In another service, on Maundy Thursday, the worship environment was beautifully designed for the congregation to sit facing one another around tables set with candles and white tablecloths. In the center was a small table with bread and a cup surrounded by

dried palm leaves, artistically arranged. Images of Christ replaced
the profusion of handbills usually posted on the bulletin board.

The service began with a footwashing ritual. The water was
cold, towels ran short, and directions were fuzzy. The hymns, which
had little to do with Maundy Thursday, were clumsily adapted for
inclusive language, and they were lengthy; we sang a slow-paced
hymn with only one stanza four times. Although the scripture readings focused on the night before Jesus died, the time for meditation
and group sharing focused on memories of persons we had known
who exemplified servanthood. Then we quickly shared Holy Communion (we heard the institution narrative, but there was no prayer
of thanksgiving) and ate a potluck meal. The service and meal had
continued so long that people began to leave before the closing
prayer, whispering in jest, "Are your feet dry yet?"

The separate parts and the leadership styles in both services
were quite good, but the way I experienced the two services con-
trasted vividly. The first excited and moved me; the second bored
and frustrated me. The difference, for me, had to do with how the
elements of each service were integrated. The first beautifully focused around the theme of new life, alluding to baptism and using
the symbol of abundant water. By avoiding mention of Jesus except
in the readings, the second service seemed not even to fit into the
day of the liturgical year we had gathered to celebrate. The parts
(hymns, readings, and reflection) did not fit together or progress
from one to the other in a way I could readily discern. Some details
had not been carefully planned. An excellent visual environment
and competent leadership did not make up for the lack of thematic
integration and coordinated planning.

No matter how much care is given to choice or composition of
the various parts of worship, worship will lose its wings and fall to
earth if the parts are not integrated. As my reflection, above, on the
two services shows, integration has several dimensions. The most
obvious dimension is the way parts—the reading and interpretation
of scripture, the hymns, the prayers, and the visual environment—
fit together and reinforce one another. A central focus related to the
congregation's reason for coming together connects the parts of the
service, as do brief transitional words between the parts. Another di-

mension of integration is proportionality. Proportion is central in visual art; the way colors and shapes are balanced with one another and placed on the canvas may be the main reason a work engages us or does not. Proportion in worship means a balance in length and feeling between different parts of the service so that leaders don't extend one part and rush through another. A sense of movement or flow is central to drama or music and to integrated worship. Consider a film that seems to be stuck too long in the same sequence. Like a hymn that is tediously long, the overlong sequence detracts from the vitality and movement of the whole. Another thing that can amaze us about art is attention to small details—a camera angle, a moving part in the bass, a swirl in the glaze of a pot. Nothing is neglected, all is attended. Perfectionism in worship deadens the human spirit; we are always afraid of getting something wrong. Careful attention to detail, however, expresses the loving, reverent care appropriate to worshiping the living God and gathering in community. Integration in worship, then, depends on relating the parts to one another in good proportion with a good sense of movement around a central focus and with careful attention to details.

To some extent, the ability to integrate dimensions of worship is a gift akin to other artistic gifts. But it is also a craft that can be learned, like using a potter's wheel, playing a scale, or learning how to show perspective in visual art. In this chapter, I give my insight into the craft of integrating worship.

Integrating the Parts
of Worship

In most cases, the text or texts for the day (selected by one of several methods described in chapter 5) will provide the integrating center for worship. I have suggested that one text be central for preaching; the same text provides a focus for other parts of the service. The call to worship or greeting may subtly echo the text; churches using the lectionary may use the psalm or Hebrew scripture for the day as the basis for a call to worship that also integrates contemporary experience. The prayer of confession may grow out of the scripture and sermon, as may the intercessions. At least one hymn may relate directly to the scripture. Anthems, too, may follow the theme of a service, through coordination with the director of music; and worship leaders may echo words from the anthem in spontaneous words of praise or prayer, weaving the anthem into the service. The benediction may echo words, themes, and images from scripture and sermon. Subtle use of key images and phrases throughout a service can integrate a worship service.

The same is true when the organizing theme of worship does not come from a scripture text. When each part relates to the whole, a sense of unity emerges.

Worship leaders should avoid repeating themes until they become pedantic. Few people are ready to focus on a theme the moment they enter a worship space; the early parts of worship may appropriately be more general. Subtlety is needed too; though integration is achieved by returning to a theme, it should not be hammered into worshipers' heads by repeating the same phrase or image over and over. I used the call to worship based on Psalm 30 given in chapter 6 when preaching about Tabitha, who served others through sewing; one phrase says, "You remove the garments of mourning and clothe us in gladness."[1] This subtly echoed the scripture we would be exploring later in the service. Mention of Tabitha too early would have been confusing, and, besides, overly explicit tie-ins soon seem pedantic and boring. As an organizing focus, an image often creates interest better than a concept does. The focusing theme should echo through a service, like a musical theme weaves through several movements of a symphony, repeated at key points, but not in every measure.

In basing materials around a theme or an image, worship planners should (as suggested in chapter 1) draw on a variety of resources, in combination with locally created words. Denominational worship books, notably the Episcopalian *Book of Common Prayer* and the Presbyterian *Book of Common Worship*, provide collects geared to the church year. Many supplemental books provide worship resources geared to the Sundays of the church year. Even churches that do not follow the lectionary can locate resources for texts they plan to use; a scripture index of the church year will direct them to a particular day of the church year in worship resource books.[2]

Denominational books and hymnals also provide prayers, such as the prayer of illumination from the *United Methodist Hymnal* found in chapter 6, that are general enough to use on any occasion. Such materials provide balance to words drawn from the theme for the day, lest the theme seem overbalanced.

Participation through the senses, and not just words, is an important part of integrated worship. Developing a theme through sound, sight, movement, smell, touch, and taste allows the whole person and the diversity of persons to participate more fully in worship. Words have more power to communicate and evoke imagination for a broad range of persons when complemented by expressions through the other senses. Liturgical art communicates more effectively when integrated with parts of a service using words. Judith Lane Chatfield, a United Church of Christ pastor and liturgical dancer, has opened the world of liturgical dance to me. Liturgical dance had never made sense to me. I could never understand what the dancers were trying to communicate; so the dance always seemed to be an ornament or intermission in the service. Chatfield approaches liturgical dance differently. She prefers to take part in planning the entire service, and whatever she does supports the rest of worship. In fact, sometimes she simply enhances movements already part of the service—such as bringing forward the elements for communion or bringing in the cross. At other times, she will interpret a scripture reading through movement after it is read. She includes opportunities for simple congregational movement (such as arm movements to "Spirit of the Living God"); this connects the congregation with the movement of the more highly trained dancer(s). Hers is not the only possible model for integrating dance into worship, as I have since learned, but it demonstrates the importance of integrating the arts into the total worship experience. The many arts of worship—fabric art, dance, music, and creative use of words—find their fullest expression and contribute most to worship when everything is carefully integrated.

Integration is also essential in honoring varied cultural traditions. One mostly English-speaking church had a practice of including something from the global church at a special time in the service; at times, they would pray the Prayer of Jesus in Spanish. The congregation prayed the same prayer in English later, following their time of intercessory prayer. How wise they were to change their practice so that they sometimes prayed the Prayer of Jesus in Spanish to close their intercessory prayer time. Placing the prayer where it belonged and integrating it into the flow of worship enabled some people to learn to pray in a new language and others to pray in their first language. Inculturation of worship is an incarnation of the challenge and comfort of the gospel in a particular culture. To be meaningful, a song from Korea, a dance from Africa, a cloth from Guatemala, or a Navajo prayer must fit the whole context and theme of worship. To incarnate the gospel in worship means to express the central meanings of a service in culturally appropriate forms.[3] To insert cultural elements that are unrelated to the rest of worship fails to honor either the culture or the experience of worship.

Obviously, integration is possible only as people involved in the various ministries of worship (music, visual art, dance, leadership of children and youth, preaching) communicate and cooperate with one another. The pastoral leadership of a church should take responsibility to make sure this happens.

Integrating worship means weaving together every means of participation (silence, the senses, spontaneity, well-known liturgies and hymns, and words prepared for the occasion) into a balanced whole.[4] The focus of a worship service is ordinarily chosen locally (even if only to decide how to celebrate Palm Sunday) and expressed through sermons and prayers prepared ahead of time. Thus, the creative voice of "prophetic verbal participation"[5] is central to the integration of worship. Yet all the parts must fit together in a meaningful flow around the focus to support vital, participatory worship.

Designing Basic
Order and Flow

Like music, worship should flow, that is, it should progress gracefully from one part to the next. When there is good progression, things happen in an understandable sequence; the service seems to be going somewhere. Through good flow, a service and its witness to faith are intelligible. Although worshipers may not consciously question why worship proceeds in a given way, they participate more fully when carried along with the movement of the service. Good flow also respects human experience and emotion. Worshipers are gently carried through feelings rather than thrown haphazardly back and forth through different feeling tones.

Although designing a good flow is to some extent an intuitive process that differs with every service, using the same good basic order every Sunday, with some flexibility, is an excellent start. The basic order for worship that is now common to many churches, Protestant and Roman Catholic, makes good theological and liturgical sense. Different denominations name the parts differently, and the order varies somewhat, but the structure that follows is representative:

1. *The community gathers in praise and thanksgiving* to God, through such things as instrumental music, an opening hymn and prayer, and a greeting or call to worship. A general act of confession (not based around the theme for the day) may come here.
2. *The community listens for the Word of God,* through the prayer for illumination, the scripture readings, and preaching. The children's sermon, if any, should go here. Contemporary experience is put in dialogue with the resources of scripture and church tradition.
3. *The community responds to the Word of God.* An invitation to discipleship or a denominational or ecumenical creed may provide an opportunity to affirm the Christian faith. An order of baptism or baptismal renewal provides a similar opportunity. Prayers of intercession for the church and the world should follow such affirmations of faith and discipleship in most services of Christian worship. The community also may respond through an act of confession or unison prayer growing out of the scripture or sermon.
4. *The community gives thanks to God,* through the sacrament of eucharist or a prayer of thanksgiving. Celebrating Holy Communion complements the preaching of the gospel, and thus some would argue that Holy Communion should

immediately follow the sermon.[6] Most denominations,
however, place Holy Communion so that it is the culmina-
tion of the congregation's response.

5. *The community is sent into the world to live as God's people.* This
   should always include both a blessing and charge, and usually an appropriate closing hymn. Closing instrumental music may follow.

One thing that distinguishes this basic order from those of the past
is the speed with which it moves to the reading and interpretation
of scripture. The more worship correlates scripture and human experience and the more it is integrated around a theme or image, the
more sense it makes to move quickly toward scripture and sermon.
The parts make more sense once the congregation members have
reflected on what is read and preached.

Many United States Protestant churches have become accustomed to having the sermon come very near the end of a service,
followed only by blessing, charge, a closing hymn, and instrumental music. Oddly enough, that pattern is a remnant of revival services and their mark on much Protestant worship in the United
States. Revival services began with prayer and singing (to open the
heart to the word), continued with preaching, and ended with an
altar call and a gospel song.[7] (They thus usually dispensed with earlier worship patterns that included Holy Communion and/or prayers
following the sermon.) Many Protestant churches adopted a similar
order for Sunday worship, perhaps only celebrating communion
quarterly. Some churches still invite people to come forward to the
front of the church for prayer, whether to make or renew their
Christian commitment or to bring their needs to God. Other Protestant churches dispensed with evangelistic preaching and the altar
call around the beginning of the twentieth century, without restor-
ing other means of responding to the gospel. In recent decades,
however, many in this second group of churches have begun to
provide a fuller response to the gospel through creeds, invitations
to Christian discipleship, and prayers. Most denominations that
once baptized in private are now insisting that baptism take place
as part of Christian worship, and many churches are celebrating

communion more frequently. Recovery of these fuller patterns of Christian worship is essential, theologically and liturgically.

To some, recovering a response to the gospel may seem to make the sermon less important, since worshipers may not leave with the words of the sermon echoing in their minds. The reverse is true; by responding in some way to a sermon's witness to the grace and challenge of the gospel, worshipers move toward integrating that witness into their lives. On the other hand, it is better to keep the response simple than to proliferate forms of response. If the service is overloaded with a broad range of responses (baptism, communion, intercessions, announcements, and other prayers), the spiritual movement of opening to God may be short-circuited.

Considering this basic flow can ease the task of designing a worship service without a preexisting structure, perhaps for a denominational meeting or a church group. Questions to ask include the following:

> How will we as a worshiping congregation begin by acknowledging God and one another?
> How will scripture and the human situation be read and interpreted?
> How will we respond?
> How will we give thanks to God?
> How will we prepare ourselves to bring what we have experienced into our daily lives?

This approach enables planners not simply to mix and match elements of a service, but to put them together with a purpose and direction.

Evaluating the Flow

The common order I have just described moves a long way toward a graceful flow in worship. Now I will suggest several criteria to consider in evaluating the flow of worship services.[8]

The way a worship service progresses is important. Each part should follow logically from the previous part and have meaning as part of the whole. Clutter should be avoided, and everything should happen for a reason. Anything that does not help movement progress should be eliminated. Often an order only makes sense because it has been used for decades; but worship committees should consider whether a newcomer unaccustomed to the order could make sense of it. Keeping similar things together helps the service progress smoothly. For example, the prayer for illumination, the scripture readings, and the sermon should be close together; if scripture is interpreted particularly for children, the children's time should come immediately after the scripture reading or sermon and relate to them. Relating the parts of worship addressed to children to the rest of worship both honors the children and supports good flow in worship.

A simple structure helps a service progress; and avoiding duplication supports simplicity. A student service featured the Apostles' Creed in three forms: as part of the call to worship, as a response to the sermon, and as part of a baptismal order. *Alluding* to the creed in the call to worship might have helped to unify the service, but saying most of it responsively there caused the service to sputter and run out of steam by the third time we said the same words.

Church leaders also can consider whether they intend the theology the service expresses. Is the starting point human experience, scripture, or tradition? How do we correlate the three? Is there room for spontaneity, the present work of the Spirit? Or is tradition and continuity valued more? Does the service center on God, on the community of faith, or on service in the world? How is relationship with God, one another, and the world expressed in a church's ordinary order of worship? What desired human response does the order assume (conversion, social action, healing of church members)? Does the order give any clue about what the church holds important and what it neglects? Would a visitor misunderstand the values of the congregation through what its worship emphasizes or neglects?

Another area for consideration is how we deal with human emotions. Zan Holmes offers one model for dealing with emotion in preaching: "Start low; go slow; go high; strike fire. Sit down."[9] This aphorism, found in other forms among African American Christians, demonstrates the wisdom of many compelling preachers. The preacher spends some time establishing a relationship with the congregation, acknowledging its leaders and others known to the preacher, and establishing the theme of the sermon. Just when one is wondering when the sermon will get going, the preacher builds in intensity and carries the congregation into an "Aha!" of naming how God is at work in their life situations, bringing both comfort and challenge. The slow pace at the beginning would be sleep-inducing if continued too long; the emotion at the sermon climax would be too intense to carry on forever; so the preacher helps the congregation return from the heights of feeling with a few quiet words that bring it all together, then sits down. In this way, the emotional flow supports the conceptual content of a sermon. Other cultural traditions (within and beyond African American contexts) might follow different models for channeling emotion in worship, but Holmes's aphorism represents one viable approach. Dealing wisely with human experience animates a sermon or a worship service.

Dealing with human emotions means avoiding abrupt changes in mood, but moving intentionally from one feeling tone to another. Two of us led worship at a faculty retreat. On the way home, another faculty member commented that the taped musical selection played at the end bothered her. I learned that she was disturbed by the upbeat, "rock" quality of the piece, immediately after a meditative communion service. We played havoc with her experience by not considering how the communion service would flow into the final song.

Wisdom about the movement of human emotions and experience through worship comes most of all from loving care in a particular context, but a few guidelines apply. In general, it is good to balance stability and variation. Some change from week to week keeps people's interest, but too much variation forces worshipers to concentrate their energy on figuring out what they are to do next, rather than on the content of worship. A relatively stable order of worship allows worshipers to follow along comfortably with the flow. On the other hand, having one or two unusual elements in a service may develop interest but not confusion. Leaders must introduce any changes in worship order carefully, with respect for people's past experiences and for local and denominational traditions.

People who ordinarily lead worship can learn much about the

human dimension in worship by occasionally participating in worship without taking a leadership role. Worship planners should consider what people may be experiencing as the service proceeds. When I was a pastor, I lived alone; but hearing about family struggles to get organized and arrive at church on time educated me about the need for centering time at the beginning of worship. Also just because the pastor has been preparing for Epiphany all week doesn't mean that every worshiper has even heard of Epiphany! Worship leaders, who may move more frequently or in ways different from the rest of the congregation, also must be sensitive to the congregation's needs to sit still or move. The flow of the service for the person in the pulpit is different from that experienced by the person in the pew. Worship planners have the responsibility to be sensitive to what worshipers might be experiencing.

Considering Proportion

Good proportion between parts of a service complements and supports good integration and flow. Although it is difficult to give precise guidelines about proportion, I can point to areas to consider. Are some parts overly long in relation to the rest of the service? Most people would agree that good proportion is jeopardized when, in a service of one hour, the sermon lasts forty-five minutes or the announcements take twenty minutes. The point is not service length, but whether enough time is given to the various parts.

Worship leaders also might ask whether there are parts of the service when people seem always to be restless (squirming, coughing, or looking at their watches)? Is this part dragging on too long? This might, for instance, lead a congregation to search for graceful ways of distributing Holy Communion more quickly. Or worship planners might consider whether worship includes enough time on each of the five basic parts outlined above to fulfill its purpose without rushing or dragging. Smaller units of the service also bear thought; one could consider whether a long or short hymn would serve the movement of worship at a given point. When things are in proportion, the content and the length of particular parts are appropriate to movement of the whole.

Caring for Detail

In describing the disciplines of writing for worship, I argued that even incorrect punctuation can interrupt people's worship. Attention or inattention to detail made a big difference in the services described at the beginning of the chapter. I am not promoting perfectionism. Years ago, I was beginning my first church as a solo pastor, and, in turn, the church was experiencing their first woman pastor. We all tiptoed around on our best behavior. I was so awed to administer communion that my hands shook. Then, one Sunday three months into my pastorate, I dropped a plate of communion bread. After the service, members of the congregation and I had a good laugh and began to relax with one another. My big mistake helped us take off our masks and become more honest with one another. We should approach worship with reverence, yet without taking ourselves too seriously. God must smile with affection at our attempts to express the unspeakable in worship. Care for detail in worship is not a search for perfectionism but an awareness that every part contributes to the whole. Those of us who express ourselves best through words must realize that some congregation members may express themselves best through movement; the cover of the bulletin will move some people more than its contents. Attention to every aspect can be time-consuming and is best done by several people with different gifts and perspectives. Many other priorities in the church's mission rightly claim leaders' attention, but vital worship energizes people for mission. Care for detail means balancing concern for the various dimensions of worship, rather than, say, putting all available energy into the sermon or hymns and neglecting the visual environment. Nurturing all these dimensions of worship demonstrates love for the worship of God and the gathering of Christian community.

The Creative Voice and
Holistic Worship

I began this book by acknowledging that the creative voice is just one dimension of vital and participatory worship. In this chapter it becomes clear that the creative voice is meaningful when all parts of worship are integrated with one another. The creative voice is important to worship, since it focuses all that is said and done in a particular service. Yet the larger focus of worship is our relationship with God, nurtured not only through the novel but also through the familiar, expressed not only through words but through all the senses. Worship may draw from wells of individual creativity, yet our openness to the Spirit is also openness to community—that words may take wing to express the praise, lament, thanksgiving, and commitment of the whole people of God. This is what it means to draw on the creative voice to find words for worship.

Notes

Chapter 1: Finding Words for Worship

1. *Pilgrim Hymnal* (Boston: The Pilgrim Press, 1958), 498–500.

2. United Church of Christ Office for Church Life and Leadership, *Book of Worship: United Church of Christ* (New York: UCC Office for Church Life and Leadership, 1986), 127–65 (hereafter cited as *Book of Worship: UCC*).

3. *Evangelical and Reformed Book of Worship* (General Synod of the Evangelical and Reformed Church, 1942), 260. According to Massey Shepherd, this prayer was compiled by George W. Douglas "from several phrases from two sermons by John Henry Newman, preached in 1842 and 1843 respectively," as well as from other sources. This version appeared in the English Proposed *Book of Common Prayer* of 1928, and later in several other worship books. Refer to Massey Shepherd, *Oxford American Prayer Book Commentary* (New York: Oxford University Press, 1950), 594–595. I am indebted to Episcopalian liturgical scholar Byron Stuhlman for locating this information for me.

4. Craig Douglas Erickson, *Participating in Worship* (Louisville, Ky.: Westminster/John Knox Press, 1989), 105.

5. Ibid., 106, 111–14.

6. Ibid., 105.

7. Elizabeth O'Connor, *Eighth Day of Creation* (Waco, Tex.: Word Books, 1971), 15.

8. Phyllis A. Bird, *The Bible as the Church's Book* (Philadelphia: Westminster Press, 1982), 16.

9. Erik Routley, *A Panorama of Christian Hymnody* (Chicago: G.I.A., 1979), 28.

10. The fact that members of the committee were experts chosen by their denominations for what was expected to be a minor revision made it more likely that the committee would be mostly male. The committee did consult with women (such as Marjorie Procter-Smith) on various issues,

such as improving the number and choice of readings related to women. The process may not reveal intentional sexism. Yet denominations that are progressive in regard to the roles of women should be intentional in ensuring that voices of women are heard in ecumenical settings.

11. This metaphor for interpreting scripture comes from Marjorie Procter-Smith, *In Her Own Rite: Constructing Feminist Liturgical Tradition* (Nashville: Abingdon Press, 1990), 122.

12. Elisabeth Schüssler Fiorenza, *Bread Not Stone: The Challenge of Feminist Biblical Interpretation* (Boston: Beacon Press, 1984), 61.

13. Elisabeth Schüssler Fiorenza, "Tablesharing and the Celebration of the Eucharist," in *Can We Always Celebrate the Eucharist?*, ed. Mary Collins and David Power, *Concilium* 152 (February 1982): 5.

14. William Beaven Abernethy and Philip Joseph Mayher, *Scripture and Imagination: The Empowering of Faith* (New York: The Pilgrim Press, 1988), 76.

15. Ibid., 40.

16. Erik Routley, "Scriptural Resonances in Hymnody," *Reformed Liturgy and Music* 16, no. 3 (summer 1982): 120–25.

17. Procter-Smith, 118.

18. Ibid., 120.

19. Ibid., 123.

20. Ibid., 124.

21. Christine M. Smith, *Weaving the Sermon: Preaching in a Feminist Perspective* (Louisville, Ky.: Westminster/John Knox Press, 1989).

Chapter 2: The Creative Process

1. Peter Elbow, *Writing with Power* (New York: Oxford University Press, 1981), 9.

2. Etty Hillesum, *From an Interrupted Life: The Diaries of Etty Hillesum, 1941–1943*, trans. Arno Pomerans (New York: Pantheon Books, 1984), 36. English translation copyright Jonathan Cape Ltd. Copyright 1981 by De Haan/Unieboek b.v., Bussum.

3. Patricia Wilson-Kastner describes a process of entering into scripture based on the teaching of Ignatius of Loyola in her book, *Imagery for Preaching* (Philadelphia: Fortress Press, 1989), 66–75.

4. Amos Wilder, *Theopoetic* (Philadelphia: Fortress Press, 1976), 2.

5. Ibid., 6.

6. Gabriele Lusser Rico, *Writing the Natural Way* (Los Angeles: J. P. Tarcher, Inc., 1983), 28–49.

7. Rebecca Ferguson developed this technique for teaching composition at Marquette University and described it to me in a personal conversation on March 19, 1994. She has been a valuable resource through her own experience and her knowledge of the literature related to creative writing.

8. Rico, *Writing the Natural Way*, 35.

9. Elbow, *Writing with Power*, 7.

10. Brian Wren, preface to *Faith Looking Forward* (Carol Stream, Ill.: Hope Publishing Company, 1983).

11. W. Thomas Smith, foreword to *Faith Looking Forward*, by Brian Wren.

Chapter 3: Disciplines of Writing for Worship

1. Fred Craddock, *Preaching* (Nashville: Abingdon Press, 1985), 92.

2. The Joint Committee on Worship (Cumberland Presbyterian Church, Presbyterian Church in the United States, The United Presbyterian Church in the United States of America), *The Worshipbook* (Philadelphia: Westminster Press, 1972), 6 (Preface) and hymn no. 626.

3. Annie Dillard, *Holy the Firm* (New York: Bantam Books, 1977), 65.

4. Ibid., 65.

5. Ibid., 60.

6. Søren Kierkegaard, *Purity of Heart Is to Will One Thing* (New York: Harper & Row, 1948), 180–81.

7. George Orwell, "Politics and the English Language," anthologized in *The Lexington Reader*, ed. Lynn Z. Bloom (Lexington, Mass.: D. C. Heath & Company, 1986), 77.

8. Ibid., 77.

9. High school cheer remembered by Carol Blair, Garrett-Evangelical Theological Seminary graduate.

10. The Episcopal Church (United States), *The Book of Common Prayer* (New York: Oxford University Press, 1984), 320 (hereafter cited as *Book of Common Prayer*).

11. Refer to the following books on grammar and style: V. A. Howard and J. H. Barton, *Thinking on Paper* (New York: William Morrow & Co., 1986); William Strunk and E. B. White, *Elements of Style*, 3d ed. (New York: Macmillan Publishing Co., 1979); and Andrea A. Lunsford and Robert Connors, *The St. Martin's Handbook* (New York: St. Martin's Press, 1989).

12. Jess Stein, ed., *The Random House College Dictionary* (New York: Random House, 1988), 915.

13. Ibid., 924.

14. Richard Carl Hoefler, *Creative Preaching and Oral Writing* (Lima, Ohio: C.S.S. Publishing Co., 1978), 116–18.

15. Janet Morley, *All Desires Known: Prayers Uniting Faith and Feminism* (New York: Morehouse-Barlow Co., 1988), 48. Wisdom of Solomon is part of the biblical canon for Roman Catholics and others.

16. The theology of Karl Barth strongly emphasizes the sovereignty and transcendence of God.

17. Martin E. Marty, "M.E.M.O.: Wondering Minds," *The Christian Century* 110, no. 14 (April 28, 1993): 471.

18. African American spiritual, "Woke Up This Morning," stanzas 1–3, as found in *Lead Me, Guide Me: The African American Catholic Hymnal* (Chicago: G.I.A. Publications, 1987), hymn no. 310.

19. Reported by Arthur Clyde at a showcase on the United Church of Christ hymnal at the annual meeting of the Hymn Society in the United States and Canada, June 28, 1994.

20. Inter-Lutheran Commission on Worship, *Lutheran Book of Worship* (Minneapolis: Augsburg Publishing House and Philadelphia: Board of Publications, Lutheran Church in America, 1978), hymn no. 165.

Chapter 4: Finding Images for Worship

1. Sources quoted in this paragraph are: the hymn attributed to Dorothy A. Thrupp; the hymn by Martin Luther, as translated by Frederick H. Hedge; John 15:5; Acts 2:3, paraphrased; typical phrase from a prayer of confession, Isaiah 53:6; a sermon by David Owens, pastor of First Congregational Church UCC, Wilmette, Illinois. It is not coincidental that I remember this sermon after several months—the vivid image kept it fresh in my memory.

2. Flora Slosson Wuellner, *Heart of Healing, Heart of Light* (Nashville: Upper Room Books, 1992), 29–39.

3. John Sanford, *Healing and Wholeness* (New York: Paulist Press, 1977), 137–38.

4. Refer to *Gender and Name of God: The Trinitarian Baptismal Formula* (New York: The Pilgrim Press, 1991) 68–69, for further discussion and references on the subject.

5. Brian Wren, "God of Many Names," in *Praising a Mystery* (Carol Stream, Ill.: Hope Publishing Company, 1986), hymn no. 8.

6. Patricia Wilson-Kastner, *Imagery for Preaching* (Philadelphia: Fortress Press, 1989), 100.

7. Christine Smith, *Weaving the Sermon* (Louisville, Ky.: Westminster/John Knox Press, 1989), 149.

8. Dennis Baron, *Grammar and Gender* (New Haven, Conn.: Yale University Press, 1986), 99.

9. Refer to Johanna W. H. van Wijk-Bos, *Reimagining God: The Case for Scriptural Diversity* (Louisville, Ky.: Westminster John Knox Press, 1995) for a discussion of the variety of images for God found in scripture.

10. Nelle Morton, *The Journey Is Home* (Boston: Beacon Press, 1985), 127–29.

11. Wilson-Kastner, *Imagery for Preaching*, 50.

12. Wren, "God of Many Names," in *Praising a Mystery*, hymn no. 8.

13. Gail Ramshaw, *Christ in Sacred Speech* (Philadelphia: Fortress Press, 1986), 9.

14. Marjorie Procter-Smith has provided "non-sexist," "inclusive," and "emancipatory" as ways to describe strategies for expressing the insights of feminist theology through liturgical language in *In Her Own Rite* (Nashville: Abingdon Press, 1990), 63. See also Smith, *Weaving the Sermon*, 75.

15. Brian Wren devotes his time to writing and to speaking about hymnody and worship. For information, write to him in care of Hope Publishing Company, Carol Stream, Ill. 60188.

Chapter 5: Finding Words to Preach

1. David Buttrick, *Homiletic* (Philadelphia: Fortress Press, 1987), 141–43.

2. Smith, *Weaving the Sermon*, 147.

3. James Forbes, *The Holy Spirit in Preaching* (Nashville: Abingdon Press, 1989), 98–105.

4. The Consultation on Common Texts, *The Revised Common Lectionary* (Nashville: Abingdon Press, 1992), 9. This book provides further explanation of lectionaries and the principles that guided development of the Revised Common Lectionary.

5. During the Sundays after Epiphany, except the last, the epistle readings are not intended to complement the other readers.

6. *The Revised Common Lectionary*, 11.

7. Justo L. González and Catherine Gunsalus González, *Liberation Preaching: The Pulpit and the Oppressed* (Nashville: Abingdon Press, 1980), 38–47.

8. Ibid., 69–93.

9. Smith, *Weaving the Sermon*, 97–98; Schüssler Fiorenza, *Bread Not Stone*, chapter 2, 23–42.

10. Examples include *Troubling Biblical Waters*, ed. Cain Hope Felder (Maryknoll, N.Y.: Orbis Books, 1989); *Voices from the Margin*, ed. R. S. Sugirtharajah (London: SPCK, 1991); and *The Women's Bible Commentary*, ed. Carol A. Newsom and Sharon H. Ringe (Louisville, Ky.: Westminster/John Knox Press, 1992).

11. It is my sense that mainline Protestants and Roman Catholics have embraced the lectionary because of a desire to engage scriptures more fully in preaching, whereas African American preachers (even if part of mainline denominations) and evangelical preachers have not followed the lectionary as readily, both because of their preference for other ways of choosing scripture and because preaching in these traditions already tended to engage scriptures more deeply.

12. Refer to Fred B. Craddock, *As One Without Authority* (Nashville: Abingdon Press, 1971), 51–76.

13. Eugene Lowry, *The Homiletical Plot* (Atlanta: John Knox Press, 1980).

14. Both teachers of preaching and congregations tend to feel strongly whether one should or should not use a manuscript in preaching. There is truth on both sides. If a manuscript is taken into the pulpit, it should be used with freedom. Its purpose is to prompt direct communication between preacher and congregation. One might also organize one's thoughts using a manuscript but take only notes into the pulpit. The message should be thought out carefully and practiced aloud, whether or not the preacher takes a manuscript, notes, chart, or outline into the pulpit. Preachers must discover for themselves what will help them achieve the goal of clear, well-organized, and direct communication with good eye-contact.

15. I learned some of these imaginative methods from Donald F. Chatfield, professor of preaching at Garrett-Evangelical Theological Seminary.

16. Richard Carl Hoefler, *Creative Preaching and Oral Writing* (Lima, Ohio: C.S.S. Publishing Co., 1978), 36–37.

17. I learned this excellent method of leading preaching feedback from Donald F. Chatfield.

Chapter 6: Forms of Prayer and Worship

1. "Presider" is a term often used to designate the primary worship leader, often but not always the pastor of a congregation. This person may not speak more than others, but supports all leaders and the congregation in their worship by giving cues or directions, coordinating leaders, and in other ways guiding their prayer. The term "presider" is also used of the main administrant(s) at communion, and it implies that while one person may preside, that person is praying on behalf of the others.

2. W. Jardine Grisbrooke, "Synaxis," in *The New Westminster Dictionary of Liturgy and Worship,* ed. J. G. Davies (Philadelphia: Westminster Press, 1986), 501 (hereafter cited as *New Westminster Dictionary*).

3. *Book of Worship: UCC,* 494.

4. When this wording of the trinitarian formula is used to begin worship, it is often called "the solemn declaration."

5. Ruth C. Duck, in *Touch Holiness: Resources for Worship,* ed. Ruth C. Duck and Maren C. Tirabassi (New York: Pilgrim Press, 1990), 77.

6. Maren C. Tirabassi, in *Touch Holiness,* 37.

7. Elsa Tamez, "Come Let Us Celebrate," in *No Longer Strangers,* ed. Iben Gjerding and Katherine Kinnamon (Geneva: WCC Publications, 1983), 20.

8. Some avoid the term "invocation" because it implies God is not among us unless we ask; others want to reserve the term for the invocation of the Holy Spirit during the eucharistic prayer.

9. Ronald J. Allen, Michael K. Kinnamon, Katherine G. Newman Kinnamon, and Keith Watkins, *Thankful Praise: A Resource for Christian Worship* (St. Louis: CBP Press, 1987), 33.

10. *Book of Worship: UCC,* 477.

11. Grisbrooke, "Collect," in *New Westminster Dictionary,* 177.

12. *The United Methodist Book of Worship* (Nashville: United Methodist Publishing House, 1992), 20. Theology and Ministry Unit, Presbyterian Church (U.S.A.), and Cumberland Presbyterian Church, *Book of Common Worship* (Louisville, Ky.: Westminster/John Knox Press, 1993), includes collects under the heading "Prayer of the Day or Opening Prayer" in its basic service; each service for the church year includes a collect following the call to worship and scripture sentences and before the opening hymn. (Cited hereafter as *United Methodist Book of Worship* and *Book of Common Worship* [Presbyterian], respectively.)

13. Grisbrooke, "Collect," 177.

14. See Daniel B. Stevick, *Language in Worship: Reflections on a Crisis* (New York: Seabury Press, 1970), 121–27.

15. *United Methodist Hymnal* (Nashville: United Methodist Publishing House, 1989), 201.

16. Morley, *All Desires Known,* 9.

17. Joint Office of Worship (Presbyterian Church, U.S. and United Presbyterian Church, U.S.A.), "Commentary: Leading the Lord's Day Service," *The Service for the Lord's Day* (Philadelphia: Westminster Press, 1984), 161.

18. *United Methodist Hymnal,* 6.

19. Allen et al., *Thankful Praise,* 35.

20. *United Methodist Book of Worship,* 461.

21. Occasionally a reading may include verses scattered throughout a chapter, in which case it would be better to say, "The scripture reading is from Romans 8," rather than "Romans 8:12–17, 26–27, and 31–39."

22. *Book of Worship: UCC,* 41.

23. Valerie Saiving, "The Human Situation: A Feminine View," in *Womanspirit Rising,* ed. Carol P. Christ and Judith Plaskow (San Francisco: Harper & Row, 1979), 25–42, esp. 37 (written in 1960 and reprinted *Womanspirit Rising*); Judith Plaskow, *Sex, Sin, and Grace: Women's Experience and the Theologies of Reinhold Niebuhr and Paul Tillich* (Lanham, Md.: University Press of America, 1980); and Mary Potter Engel, "Evil, Sin, and the Violation of the Vulnerable," in *Lift Every Voice: Constructing Christian Theologies from the Underside,* ed. Susan Brooks Thistlethwaite and Mary Potter Engel (San Francisco: Harper & Row, 1990), 152–64. See also my article, "Sex, Sin, and Gender in Free-Church Protestant Worship," in *Women at Worship: Interpretations of North American Diversity,* ed. Marjorie Procter-Smith and Janet Walton (Louisville, Ky.: Westminster/Knox Press, 1993), 55–69.

24. Andrew Sung Park, *The Wounded Heart of God: The Asian Concept of Han and the Christian Doctrine of Sin* (Nashville: Abingdon Press, 1993).

25. *Book of Common Prayer*, 360.

26. *United Methodist Book of Worship*, 35.

27. Ibid.

28. *Book of Common Worship*, (Presbyterian), 343.

29. Duck, written for this book.

30. In Lucien Deiss, *Springtime of the Liturgy* (Collegeville, Minn.: Liturgical Press, 1979), 92–93.

31. Ibid., 82–85.

32. Walter C. Huffman, *Prayer of the Faithful: Understanding and Creatively Leading Corporate Intercessory Prayer* (Minneapolis: Augsburg Fortress, 1986), 27. Huffman's book was most helpful in formulating my ideas in this section, though the information is readily available enough that I do not cite Huffman's book often.

33. Richard Mazziota, *We Pray to the Lord* (Notre Dame, Ind.: Ave Maria Press, 1984).

34. E. C. Whitaker, "Bidding Prayer," in *New Westminster Dictionary*, 91–2.

35. Mazziota, op. cit., 20, quoted in Huffman, op. cit., 54–56.

36. Huffman, *Prayer of the Faithful*, 42.

37. John Allyn Melloh and William G. Storey, eds., *Praise God in Song* (Chicago: G.I.A., 1979), 271.

38. Mark R. Francis, *Liturgy in a Multicultural Community* (Collegeville, Minn.: Liturgical Press, 1991), 60.

39. "Creating Vibrant Churches: A Sermon," *The Chicago Theological Seminary Register* 84 (winter 1994): 13.

40. Refer to Deiss, *Springtime of the Liturgy*, 93.

41. James F. White, *Protestant Worship: Traditions in Transition* (Louisville, Ky.: Westminster/John Knox Press, 1989), 183.

42. Doug Adams, *Meeting House to Camp Meeting* (Saratoga, San Jose, Calif.: Modern Liturgy—Resource Publications, 1981 and Austin, Tex.: Sharing Co., 1981), 23 and passim.

43. Catherine Marshall, *The Prayers of Peter Marshall* (Lincoln, Va.: Chosen Books, 1949, new edition distributed by Waco, Tex,: Word Books, 1979), 4; discussion by Garrett-Evangelical Theological Seminary faculty, October 26, 1994.

44. Harry Emerson Fosdick, *A Book of Public Prayers* (New York: Harper & Brothers, 1959), 7.

45. For example, refer to Raymond Abba, *Principles of Christian Worship* (New York and London: Oxford University Press, 1960), 85–116.

46. Linda Vogel, faculty discussion, October 26, 1994.

47. *United Methodist Book of Worship*, 445.

48. Allen et al., *Thankful Praise*, 42.

49. Refer to Phyllis Cole and Everett Tilson, *Litanies and Other Prayers for the Revised Common Lectionary, Year A* (Nashville: Abingdon Press, 1992) and companion volumes for Years B and C for examples of "prayers for one voice" related to every Sunday in the lectionary.

50. George Arthur Buttrick, *Prayer* (Nashville: Abingdon-Cokesbury Press, 1942), 284.

51. Refer to previously cited books by Fosdick and Marshall, as well as W.E.B. DuBois, *Prayers for Dark People* (Amherst: University of Massachusetts Press, 1980), for excellent examples of pastoral prayers, which, of course, do not reflect the concern today for inclusive language.

52. George Buttrick, *Prayer,* 269.

53. Joint Office on Worship, *The Service for the Lord's Day,* 157.

54. *Book of Common Worship* (Presbyterian), 78. Scripture references cited are 1 Cor. 16:13; 2 Tim. 2:1; Eph. 6:10; 1 Thess. 5:13–22; and 1 Peter 2:17.

55. Abridged from *Book of Worship: UCC,* 501.

56. *Book of Common Worship* (Presbyterian), 78.

57. Ibid., 161.

58. Diane Karay [Tripp], *All the Seasons of Mercy* (Philadelphia: Westminster Press, 1987), 133.

59. *Book of Worship: UCC,* 116–17.

Chapter 7: Thanksgiving at Table

1. Some parts of the eucharistic prayer have been reserved for clergy— in the Western church, the institution narrative; in the Eastern church, the *epiclesis,* or invocation of the Spirit. I find the Eastern argument to be more persuasive: laity should certainly be able to tell the stories of Jesus, but clergy, as representative ministers of the whole community, might appropriately pray for the Spirit on behalf of the community. For laity and clergy to share the words and actions of communion, with clergy oversight, would be even better, since it honors the unity and diversity of ministries. Theologically, I cannot defend reserving any particular part of the communion service for clergy, for three reasons: (1) I do not find it helpful to identify a "magic moment" during the service that is more holy than others; the sacrament is sacrament because of words, actions, symbols, the community, and the presence of God. Thus there is no one moment that should require clergy leadership. (2) I feel that the proper role of clergy is to provide ongoing leadership for Holy Communion by overseeing and educating congregations about the words, actions, and symbols of the sacrament. The clergy then fulfill their role in passing on Christian traditions; this role of oversight and education is more important than who says which words. (3) As Edward Schillebeeckx has argued in *Ministry, Leadership in the Community of Jesus Christ* (New York: Crossroad, 1981), the ability of a community to

celebrate communion should take priority over the requirement that clergy preside, whether to address either a shortage of clergy in a geographical area or the unavailability of clergy for a particular occasion. Given these three reasons, I advocate further reflection within denominations about the relation of ordination and the sacraments, without encouraging congregations to depart unilaterally from their denomination's requirements.

2. Practices in the Christian Church (Disciples of Christ), where Holy Communion is celebrated weekly, provide a challenging contrast to other denominations mentioned above. Traditionally, laity, not clergy, have said the prayers at the table, usually two brief, extemporaneous prayers, one over the bread and one over the cup. These practices challenge clergy dominance of the sacrament and overdependence on long printed communion prayers. Today, some Disciples are considering whether sharing the prayers between laity and clergy could also model mutuality. They are exploring options for prayer at the table that draw more fully on ecumenical and historical models, such as those offered in this chapter. The ecumenical church could in turn learn from the Disciples of Christ that laity can take a significant role in leading Holy Communion and that locally prepared prayer can have a place at the table of Jesus Christ. Refer to Allen et al., *Thankful Praise*, 46–53.

3. Refer to *Book of Worship: UCC*, 49; and the *Book of Common Worship* (Presbyterian), 156.

4. *Book of Common Prayer* (1979), 400–405.

5. John Barry Ryan, "Eucharistic Prayers," in *New Dictionary of Sacramental Worship*, ed. Peter E. Fink (Collegeville, Minn.: Liturgical Press, 1990), 453.

6. Frank Senn, conversation with the author, August 2, 1994. Senn is a liturgical scholar who is pastor of Immanuel Lutheran Church in Evanston, Illinois. Refer also to Gail Ramshaw-Schmidt, "Toward Lutheran Eucharistic Prayers," in *New Eucharistic Prayers* ed. Frank C. Senn, (Mahwah, N.J.: Paulist Press, 1987), 74–79.

7. Words adapted by David Edwards, "When You Do This, Remember Me," in *Chalice Hymnal Sampler* (St. Louis: Chalice Press, 1993), hymn no. 26.

8. *Book of Worship: UCC*, 44.

9. First Church in Cambridge (Massachusetts)—Congregational, United Church of Christ, unpublished and untitled booklet of worship orders, 1986.

10. W. Jardine Grisbrooke, "Anaphora," in *New Westminster Dictionary*, 18.

11. "The Apostolic Tradition," chap. 4, in *Hippolytus: A Text for Students*, trans. Geoffrey J. Cuming (Bramcote, Nottinghamshire, England: Grove Books, 1976), 10–11, 21–22, set in sense lines for ease in reading.

12. This sentence is from the *Book of Worship: UCC*, 69.

13. *Book of Worship: UCC*, 46. This version of the Sanctus adapts tradi-

tion, using "God" where most orders say "Lord" and "the one" for "him." Note that in the eucharistic prayer "Blessed is the one" or "Blessed is he" refers to Jesus Christ, so this adaptation is more appropriate than some that change the phrase to "blessed are they."

14. Sometimes another person, clergy or lay, assists in saying part of the prayer.

15. *Our Passion for Justice* (New York: Pilgrim Press, 1984), 254.

16. Justin Martyr, "The First Apology of Justin, The Martyr", ed. and trans. Edward Rochie Hardy, in *The LIbrary of Christian Classics: Early Christian Fathers,* ed., Cyril C. Richardson, Vol. 1 (Philadelphia: Westminster Press, 1953), 287.

17. *United Methodist Book of Worship,* 36–38, 46–80, 124–126, 152–153.

18. Morley, *All Desires Known,* 36–45.

19. Written by Ruth Duck for this book. Refer to *Book of Common Worship* (Presbyterian), 152, for another short version of the prayer.

Chapter 8: Finding Words to Sing

1. *United Methodist Hymnal,* hymn no. 525.

2. Ibid., hymn no. 519.

3. James Rawlings Sydnor, *Hymns and Their Uses* (Carol Stream, Ill.: Agape, 1982).

4. Donald Hustad, a sympathetic observer, has noted (in an address to the Hymn Society in the United States and Canada meeting in Maryville, Tennessee, on June 29, 1994) that contemporary Christian music and scripture choruses are rather limited in subject matter. He observes that some congregations who prefer these musical styles sing only words of praise, an important but not the only dimension of Christian faith experience.

5. Austin Lovelace, *The Anatomy of Hymnody* (Chicago: G.I.A., 1965), 104.

6. Gracia Grindal reports that Renaissance poet Sir Philip Sidney paraphrased psalms as a devotional exercise. Dan Damon, a contemporary hymn writer, also writes hymns as part of his spiritual discipline.

7. Quoted in *Guide to the Pilgrim Hymnal,* by Albert C. Ronander and Ethel K. Porter (Philadelphia: United Church Press, 1966), 309.

8. Thomas H. Troeger, "Personal, Cultural, and Theological Influences on the Language and Hymns of Worship," in *The Hymn* 38 (October 1987): 10.

9. Julia Cameron, *The Artist's Way* (New York: Jeremy P. Tarcher/ Perigee, 1992), 174. This workbook helps people develop their creativity through both concepts and practical exercises.

10. Measures are divisions in music according to a rhythmic pulse. At the beginning of hymns is a time signature. HYFRYDOL (the tune printed here with "Love Divine") is in 3/4 time signature. That means there are

three quarter notes in a measure. BEECHER is in 4/4 time; there are four quarter notes in a measure. In 4/4 time, a whole note takes up a whole measure, because it is held as long as four quarter notes.

11. Gracia Grindal, *Lessons in Hymnwriting* (Fort Worth, Tex.: Hymn Society, 1986, 1991), 11.

12. Ibid.

13. Clement Wood, *The Complete Rhyming Dictionary and Poet's Craft Book* (Garden City, N.Y.: Garden City Books, 1936), 25. The introduction to Wood's book is invaluable, suggesting many more nuances of rhythm and rhyme than I can include in this volume.

14. Ibid., 25.

15. Lovelace, *Anatomy of Hymnody*, 19.

16. Wood, *Complete Rhyming Dictionary*, 32.

17. Example from Grindal, *Lessons in Hymnwriting*, 19.

18. Most of Lovelace's book *The Anatomy of Hymnody* analyses how different meters support various purposes and feeling tones of texts.

19. The Hymn Society in the United States and Canada sponsors an annual meeting of persons who write hymn tunes and texts, who compile and publish hymnals, or who love to learn new hymns. The Society publishes a journal, *The Hymn*, that explores hymns, past and present, in a scholarly yet accessible way. I would encourage Christians who would like to learn about hymns (and how to publish them) to join. (Write: The Hymn Society at Texas Christian University, P. O. Box 30854, Fort Worth, TX 76129.)

Chapter 9: Bringing It All Together

1. Duck, in *Touch Holiness*, 77.

2. *The New Handbook of the Christian Year*, ed. Hoyt L. Hickman, Don E. Saliers, Laurence Hull Stookey, and James F. White, rev. ed. (Nashville: Abingdon Press, 1992) includes such an index on pages 296–300. This is the book of resources for the church year that I would recommend most highly, because of its comprehensiveness. It suggests hymns for each Sunday, offers services for particular occasions (for instance, an Advent Service of Lessons and Carols and an Easter Vigil service), and provides an excellent brief survey of the history and theology of the church year.

3. Refer to Anscar Chupungco, *Cultural Adaptation of the Liturgy* (Ramsey, N.J.: Paulist Press, 1982), for more on the history and theology of integrating culture and worship.

4. Erickson, *Participating in Worship*, 180–193.

5. Ibid., 104–26.

6. Refer to John Riggs, "A Normative Shape for Christian Worship," *Prism: A Theological Forum of the United Church of Christ* 3, no. 2 (fall 1988): 39–41.

7. James F. White, *Protestant Worship: Traditions in Transition* (Louisville, Ky.: Westminster/John Knox Press, 1989), 177.

8. I am indebted to James F. White, "The Service of the Word," chap. 5 in *Introduction to Christian Worship*, rev. ed. (Nashville: Abingdon Press, 1990), in this section.

9. Quoted by William B. McClain in *Come Sunday* (Nashville: Abingdon Press, 1990), 68.

Acknowledgments

Grateful acknowledgment is made for permission to reprint from the following:

The text of stanza 3 of "Holy, Holy, Holy," LBW 165, *Lutheran Book of Worship*, copyright © 1978. Reprinted by permission of Augsburg Fortress.

Selected excerpts from the text of "God of Many Names," by Brian Wren, copyright © 1986. Used by permission of Hope Publishing Company, Carol Stream, Ill. 60188.

Selected excerpts from the *Book of Worship: United Church of Christ*, copyright © 1986, United Church of Christ Office for Church Life and Leadership, New York.

Lines from a eucharistic prayer in chapter 4, "The Apostolic Tradition," in *Hippolytus: A Text for Students*, trans. Geoffrey J. Cuming, copyright © 1976. Used by permission of Grove Books, Bramcote, Nottinghamshire, England.

Excerpts on commissioning and benediction by Mary Ann Neeval in "Bread for the Journey: Resources for Worship," ed. Ruth C. Duck, copyright © 1981. Used by permission of The Pilgrim Press.

Selections from the Presbyterian Church (U.S.A.) *Book of Common Worship*, copyright © 1993. Used by permission of Westminster/John Knox Press, Louisville, Ky.

Excerpt from *Springtime of the Liturgy: Liturgical Texts of the First Four Centuries*, by Lucien Deiss, copyright © 1979. Used by permission of Liturgical Press, Collegeville, Minn.

Excerpts from *The United Methodist Book of Worship*, copyright © 1992. Used by permission of United Methodist Publishing House, Nashville, Tenn.

Excerpt from *Thankful Praise: A Resource for Christian Worship*, by Ronald J. Allen, Michael K. Kinnamon, Katherine G. Newman Kinnamon, and Keith Watkins, copyright © 1987. Used by permission of Christian Board of Publication Press, St. Louis.

Selected prayers from *All Desires Known: Prayers Uniting Faith and Feminism*, by Janet Morley. Copyright © 1988 by Janet Morley. Published by SPCK, London. Used by permission of Morehouse Publishing, Harrisburg, Penn.

The poem "Come Let Us Celebrate the Supper of the Lord," by Elsa Tamez in *No Longer Strangers*, ed. Iben Gjerding and Katherine Kinnamon, copyright © 1983. Used by permission of World Council of Churches Publications, Geneva, Switzerland.